MUSIC
FOR
SIGHT SINGING

Will

MUSIC
FOR
SIGHT SINGING

Seventh Edition

ROBERT W. OTTMAN

Emeritus
College of Music
University of North Texas

NANCY ROGERS

College of Music
Florida State University

PEARSON
Prentice
Hall

Upper Saddle River, New Jersey 07458

President, Humanities/Social Sciences: *Yolanda de Rooy*
Editor-in-Chief: *Sarah Touborg*
Executive Editor: *Richard Carlin*
Editorial Assistant: *Jeanmarie Ensor*
Director of Marketing: *Brandy Dawson*
Assistant Marketing Manager: *Andrea Messineo*
Director of Production and Manufacturing: *Barbara Kittle*
Senior Managing Editor: *Lisa Iarkowski*
Production Liaison: *Joe Scordato*
Production Assistant: *Marlene Gassler*
Manufacturing Manager: *Nick Sklitsis*
Manufacturing Buyer: *Ben Smith*
Cover Design Director: *Jayne Conte*
Cover Designer: *Bruce Kenselaar*
Cover Image: *Una Formella della Cantoria of Luca Della Robbia. Florence. Museo di S. Maria del Fiore. Erich Lessing/Art Resource, NY*
Composition/Full-Service Management: *Stratford Publishing Services/Kerry Reardon*
Printer/Binder: *The Courier Companies*
Cover Printer: *Phoenix Color Corp*

Credit and acknowledgments borrowed from other sources and reproduced, with permission, in this textbook appear on appropriate page within text (or on pages xix-xx).

Pearson Education LTD.
Pearson Education Singapore, Pte. Ltd
Pearson Education, Canada, Ltd
Pearson Education—Japan

Pearson Education Australia PTY, Limited
Pearson Education North Asia Ltd
Pearson Education de Mexico, S.A. de C.V.
Pearson Education Malaysia, Pte. Ltd

1 0 9 8 7 6 5
ISBN 0-13-187234-6

CONTENTS

PART III
MELODY: CHROMATICISM
RHYTHM: FURTHER RHYTHMIC PRACTICES

PREFACE

Developing the "mind's ear"—the ability to imagine how music sounds without first playing it on an instrument—is essential to any musician, and sight singing (in conjunction with ear training and other studies in musicianship) is invaluable in reaching this fundamental goal. The principal objective of sight singing is acquiring the ability to sing a given melody accurately at *first sight*. Although repeating a melody and correcting any errors is beneficial, we can truly sight sing a melody only once, which is why *Music for Sight Singing* provides a generous number of exercises (more than 1,300 in this volume) for practice.

Generations of musicians have valued *Music for Sight Singing* for its abundance of meticulously organized melodies drawn from the literature of composed music and a wide range of the world's folk music. Not only is "real music" more enjoyable and interesting to sing than dry exercises, but genuine repertoire naturally introduces a host of important musical considerations beyond pitch and rhythm (including dynamics, accents, articulations, slurs, repeat signs, and tempo markings). The book's systematic arrangement of exercises according to specific melodic and rhythmic features lays an effective foundation for success. Each chapter methodically introduces elements one at a time, steadily increasing in difficulty while providing a musically meaningful framework around which students can hone their skills. Through this method, the book creates a sense of challenge rather than frustration: a conscientious student should always be prepared to tackle the next melody.

The text as a whole is divided into four parts:

1. Chapters 1–9, diatonic melodies with rhythmic patterns limited to whole beats and their most basic divisions (two notes per beat in simple meters, three notes per beat in compound meters)
2. Chapters 10–12, diatonic melodies with rhythmic patterns that include subdivisions of the beat (four notes per beat in simple meters, six notes per beat in compound meters)
3. Chapters 13–19, chromaticism, tonicization, modulation, and more advanced rhythmic patterns and metrical concepts
4. Chapters 20–21, modal and post-tonal music

Music for Sight Singing contains exercises appropriate for students of all skill levels, including beginners, but a basic working knowledge of fundamental music theory and notation is prerequisite to sight singing. The following abilities are particularly important:

- Recognize, write, and sing all major and minor scales
- Recognize and write all major and minor key signatures
- Recognize and write all common note values and their corresponding rests
- Recognize and interpret standard meter signatures

Each of the above will be reviewed as topics are introduced throughout the text. However, a practical command of these basic elements from the outset will ensure satisfactory progress.

A new edition of *Music for Sight Singing* offers the opportunity to build on the book's strengths, address any weaknesses, and introduce some new ideas. As always, exercises have been selected from a wide musical repertoire, and melodies written especially for pedagogical purposes are kept to a minimum. The significant revisions in the seventh edition fall into three categories:

- Expanding the purely rhythmic exercises
- Increasing the number of post-tonal melodies and improving the book's transition from tonality to atonality
- Including structured improvisation exercises in most chapters

Recognizing that it takes considerable experience to develop a genuine "feel" for rhythm and meter, the seventh edition of *Music for Sight Singing* contains 30 percent more rhythmic exercises than did the sixth edition. This expansion will be particularly noticeable in Chapters 4, 10, and 15, which respectively introduce compound meters, the subdivided beat, and syncopation—topics that many students find especially challenging. The new exercises progress more gradually from relatively easy to complicated patterns, providing students of all skill levels with ample exercises for both practice and true sight reading.

To smooth the difficult transition from tonal to post-tonal materials, *Music for Sight Singing*'s discussion of twentieth-century music (Chapter 21) has been expanded and reorganized. The early exercises in this unit focus on extensions to the familiar tonal system through melodies that push the limits of tonality or shift abruptly from one diatonic collection to another. The next set of melodies introduces whole-tone and octatonic scales— distinctive and aurally salient collections have been employed extensively by various twentieth-century composers. These two sections will help students develop a flexible strategy that judiciously combines a purely interval-based approach with an awareness of a familiar background collection, better preparing them for the more freely post-tonal and twelve-tone melodies later in the chapter.

The change in this edition that will be most noticeable to readers already familiar with *Music for Sight Singing* is the addition of structured improvisation exercises, which provide students with a framework around which to create their own melodies. These singing exercises are crafted to reinforce the lessons of their respective chapters, fundamentally emphasizing the book's organization and approach through a new kind of activity. Structured improvisation training offers specific musical and pedagogical benefits, from helping beginning students master an unfamiliar solmization system (by concentrating specifically on scale degrees and their corresponding syllables without the additional mental burden of notation) to fostering a deep awareness of harmony in students at all levels. Finally, improvisational exercises will provide additional variety to class and individual practice, and (unlike traditional sight singing) they will extend the same benefits even after multiple repetitions.

I am strongly committed to maintaining the tradition of excellence that Robert Ottman established more than 50 years ago. The combination of his vast knowledge of the repertoire and his deep pedagogical instincts made *Music for Sight Singing* one of the most celebrated music textbooks of the twentieth century. It is humbling to walk in such giant footsteps, but of course it is also a tremendous privilege to continue Dr. Ottman's work for the benefit of twenty-first-century musicians.

Nancy Rogers

IN MEMORIAM

Musicians around the world have been touched by Robert Ottman. Hundreds of fortunate students studied with him during his long career at the University of North Texas, where he is fondly remembered as an exceptionally fine and dedicated teacher. He was an inspirational role model for those who later became educators and were able to pass along his words of wisdom, his teaching techniques, and his high standards to thousands of their own students. Countless other musicians have benefited from the insight and experience that he poured into *Music for Sight Singing* and 10 other textbooks.

Dr. Ottman earned his bachelor's and master's degrees from the Eastman School of Music (1938 and 1944), then enlisted in the U.S. Army as a chaplain's assistant. During World War II, he played a portable organ during worship services and drove the chaplain's Jeep (sometimes at night, without headlights) near enemy territory in order to draw fire and pinpoint troop locations. After the war ended, he studied at Trinity College of Music in London, then returned to the United States to head the music theory department at the University of North Texas (known at the time as the North Texas State College). He received his doctorate from UNT in 1956—the same year that he published the first edition of *Music for Sight Singing.*

Serving both as a professor of music theory and as director of the Madrigal Singers, Robert Ottman was a valued member of the University of North Texas faculty throughout his 35 years there. Even after his retirement in 1981, he remained actively involved with the university and the larger Denton community. In 2004 he received the UNT President's Citation for outstanding service.

Dr. Ottman was beloved by those who knew him and, remarkably, even by people acquainted solely with his books. If it is, indeed, possible to be immortalized through one's work, then Robert Ottman will live forever in the hearts and minds of musicians all around the world.

Robert William Ottman
May 3, 1914–June 30, 2005

ACKNOWLEDGMENTS

The following publishers have granted permission to use melodies from their publications, for which the authors wish to express their appreciation. Additional acknowledgments will be found immediately below individual melodies.

Mary O. Eddy, author of *Ballads and Songs from Ohio*, published by J.J. Augustin, Locust Valley, NY: melodies 3.40, 9.20 and 11.12.

American Book Company, New York: melody 2.29 from *Songs and Pictures*, Book I, by Robert Foresman.

The American Folklore Society, Philadelphia, PA: melodies 6.47, 12.16, 13.6 and 17.69 from *Spanish-American Folk Songs*, ed. Eleanor Hague; melodies 3.35 and 20.8 from *The Journal of American Folk Lore*.

Ascherberg, Hopwood, and Crew, Ltd.: melody 4.30 from *Folk Songs of the North-Countries* by Frank Kidson; melody 8.10 from *A Garland of English Folk Songs* by Frank Kidson.

Associated Music Publishers, Inc., New York, NY: melodies 17.29 and 17.53 from *Folk Dance Music of the Slavic Nations* by H. A. Schimmerling; melodies 3.9, 3.14, 3.16, 3.28, 5.26, and 17.63 from *Das Lied der Volker* by Heinrich Möller, copyright by B. Schott's Soehne, Mainz, used by permission of the copyright owner and its agent, Associated Music Publishers, Inc.

C.F. Peters Corporation, New York, NY: melodies 3.3, 3.61, 6.18, 6.39, and 8.1 from *Deutschland in Volkslied*, ed. Gustav Kniep, copyright C. F. Peters, reprinted with permission.

Columbia University Press, New York, NY: melody 4.74 from *A Song Catcher in the Southern Mountains* by Dorothy Scarborough; melodies 3.31, 3.50, 3.63, 12.44, 15.72, 16.50, 16.68, 17.49 and 17.73 from *Folk Music and Poetry of Spain and Portugal* by Kurt Schindler, courtesy of Hispanic Institute, Columbia University.

G. Schirmer, Inc., New York, NY: melody 15.77 from *Anthology of Ialian Song by A. Parisotti*; melodies 6.48 and 13.2 from *44 French Songs and Variants* by Julian Tiersot; melody 6.27 from *Reliquary of English Song*; melody 4.87 from *Songs of Italy* by E. Marzo.

Gesellschaft zur Herausgabe von Denkmäler der Tonkunst in Osterreiech, Vienna: melodies 13.5 and 14.46 from *Denkmäler der Tonkunst in Osterreich*.

H.W. Gray Co., New York, NY: melodies 3.47, 5.15, and 12.51 from *Folk Song Chanteys and Singing Games* by Charles Farnsworth and Cecil Sharp, reprinted by permission of Novello & Co., Ltd.

Harvard University Press, Cambridge, MA: melody 15.82, reprinted by permission of the publishers from Willi Apel and Archibald T. Davison, *Historical Anthology of Music*, Vol. II, copyright 1946, 1949, 1950 by the President and Fellows of Harvard College.

Louisiana State University Press, Baton Rouge: melody 6.11 from *Louisiana-French Folk Songs* by Irene Whitfield.

Novello & Company, Ltd., London: melody 17.66 from *Caractacus* by Sir Edward Elgar, reproduced by permission; melody 20.32 from *O Lovely Babe* by Alec Rowley, reproduced by permission.

University of Alabama Press: melodies 8.24 and 15.118 from *Folk Songs of Alabama* by Byron Arnold.

University of Arizona Press: melodies 15.102 and 16.38 from *Canciones de Mi Padre* (Vol. XVII, No. 1) by Luisa Espinel, by permission.

University of Utah Press, Salt Lake City: melody 16.61 from *Ballads and Songs from Utah* by Lester A. Hubbard, University of Utah Press, 1961.

Vermont Printing Company, Brattleboro: melody 17.54 from *Cancionero Español* by Maria Diez de Onate.

I would like to thank the following individuals for their helpful suggestions as they reviewed earlier versions of this manuscript: David Kopp, Boston University; W. Ronald Clemmons, University of Alabama; Laurdella Foulkes-Levy, University of Mississippi; William Lake, Bowling Green University; John Bauer, University of Memphis; Frank Riddick, Oklahoma City University; Gordon Sly, Michigan State University; Stefan Kostka, University of Texas.

I am particularly grateful to Lisa Iarkowski, senior managing editor for humanities and social sciences at Prentice Hall, and Kerry Reardon, production editor at Stratford Publishing, for their help in preparing the manuscript for this edition. I would also like to thank Richard Carlin, executive editor for music at Prentice Hall, as well as Chris Johnson, who assisted me as executive editor when this project was in its early stages. Alexander Sanchez-Béhar provided valuable assistance obtaining permission to use the copyrighted melodies in this edition. Last but by no means least, I am enormously indebted to my husband, Michael Buchler, for his unfailing personal and professional support.

Nancy Rogers

I

RHYTHM

simple meters;
the beat and its division into two parts

An important attribute of the accomplished musician is the ability to "hear mentally"—that is, to know how a given piece of music sounds without recourse to an instrument. Sight singing, together with ear training and other studies in musicianship, helps develop that attribute. The goal of sight singing is the ability to sing *at first sight*, with correct rhythm and pitch, a piece of music previously unknown to the performer. Accomplishing that goal demonstrates that the music symbols on paper were comprehended mentally before being performed. In contrast, skill in reading music on an instrument often represents an ability to interpret music symbols as fingerings, with no way of demonstrating prior mental comprehension of the score.

To help you become proficient in sight singing, this text provides you with many carefully graded music examples. Beginning in this chapter, you will perform the simplest of exercises in reading rhythm, after which you will perform easy melodic lines that incorporate those same rhythmic patterns.

RHYTHMIC READING

In simple meters (also known as simple time), the beat is divisible into two equal parts; therefore, any note value so divisible can represent the beat. Most commonly used are the quarter note $\left(\downarrow = \eighthbeam\right)$, the eighth note $\left(\eighth = \sixteenthbeam\right)$, and the half note $\left(\half = \downarrow\,\downarrow\right)$, though other values $\left(\whole, \eighth, \sixteenth\right)$ are sometimes seen. In this chapter, the note value representing the simple division of the beat (that is, half of the beat) will be the shortest note value used. In reading, follow these suggestions:

1. *Rhythmic syllables.* Accurate rhythmic reading is best accomplished through the use of spoken or sung rhythmic syllables. Clapping and tapping are less desirable for a variety of reasons; for instance, dynamics and sustained notes are more easily performed vocally, faster tempos are possible, and vocalizing leaves the hands free for conducting. There are a variety of good rhythmic syllable systems in current use. Several popular systems are illustrated below, although you may wish to use another approach.

   a. Any note falling on a beat is given one syllable (such as *du*), and any note falling halfway between beats (that is, on the "offbeat") is given another syllable (such as *de*, pronounced "day").

   b. Any note falling on a beat is named by the beat number, and any note falling halfway between beats (that is, on the "offbeat") is pronounced *and*.

   c. Any note falling on a beat is named by the beat number, and all other notes are given the same neutral syllable (such as *ta*).

   If a note is held into the next beat, simply hold the same syllable through the note's entire duration. Because a rest indicates silence, it is customary to make no sound.

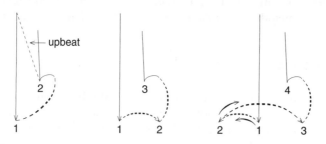

a.	du	du	du	du	du _____	du	de du	de	du _	de		du		du	
b.	1	2	3	4	1 _____	1	and 2	and	3 _	and		1		3	
c.	1	2	3	4	1 _____	1	ta 2	ta	3 _	ta		1		3	

2. *The conductor's beat.* It should be obvious that only the *first* performance of an exercise can be considered reading at *first* sight. (After that, you are practicing!) Therefore, on the first try, you should not stop to correct errors or to study what to do next. To help you complete an exercise without hesitation, the use of conductor's beats is highly recommended. Shown below are hand-movement patterns for two beats, three beats, and four beats per measure. Successive downbeats of each pattern coincide with successive bar lines.

The Conductor's Beats: two beats, three beats, and four beats per measure

The *downbeat* (1) drops in a straight line and describes a small bounce at the instant the first beat occurs. The first downbeat is preceded by an *upbeat*, beginning at the point of the last beat of the pattern being used. Therefore, the last beat of each measure is the upbeat for the following measure.

Practice these three conductor's beats without reading or singing. Next, with the left hand, tap twice for each beat of the conductor's beat. These taps represent the normal simple division of the beat-note value. When you no longer have to concentrate on these hand movements, you are ready to begin rhythmic reading and sight singing.

As you read an exercise, use the conductor's beat and tapping to keep going without pause until the very end. If you make a mistake, don't hesitate or stop; the next "1" (downbeat) will be the next bar line where you can pick up your reading and continue to the end. If you made errors or lost your place, you can review and practice in anticipation of doing better on the next exercise. Follow this procedure beginning with the very first exercises. Conducting and tapping easy exercises *now* is the best way to prepare yourself for the more difficult exercises to follow.

3. *Notation for rhythmic reading.* Exercises such as that at *a* below are designed specifically for rhythmic reading. In each, the notation is placed on a one-line staff, to avoid possible confusion when notation is on a five-line staff. However, reading rhythmic notation from a melodic line, as in example *b*, should begin as soon as possible. As seen in this pair of examples, there is no difference in the resulting performance.

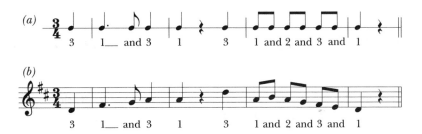

The melodies of Chapters 2 and 3 include only the same type of rhythm patterns found in Chapter 1.

Section 1. The quarter note as the beat unit. Beat-note values and larger only: ♩ = 1 beat, ♩ = 2 beats, ♩. = 3 beats, o = 4 beats.

Not all exercises begin on the first beat of the measure. Determine the beat number of the first note before reading.

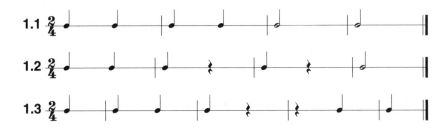

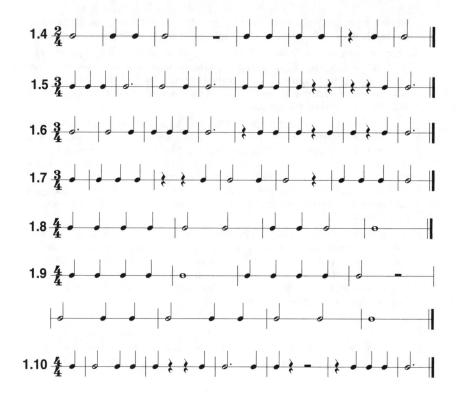

Section 2. The quarter note as the beat unit and its division ($\quarternote = \eighthnote\eighthnote$). Dotted notes and tied notes.

1___ 2 and

4

1.16

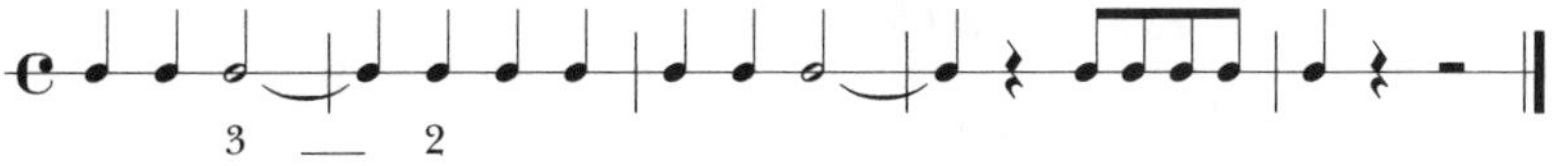

1.17

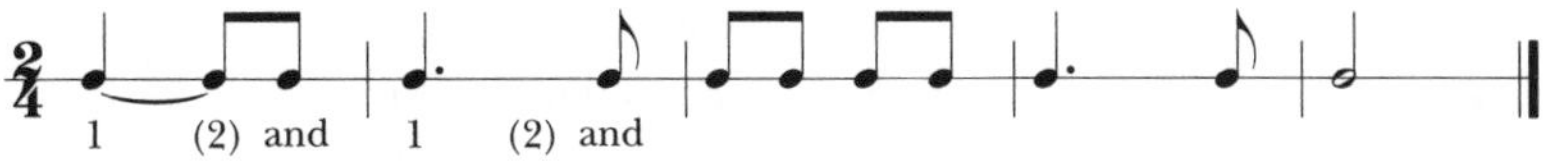

1.18

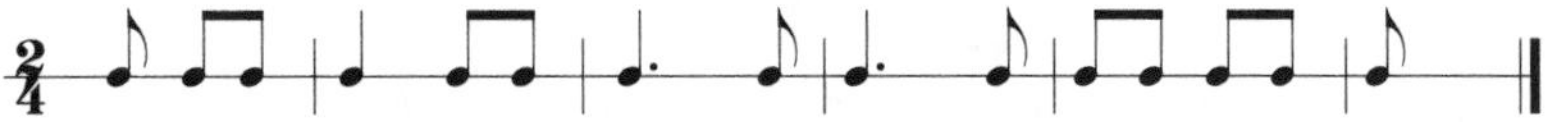

1.19

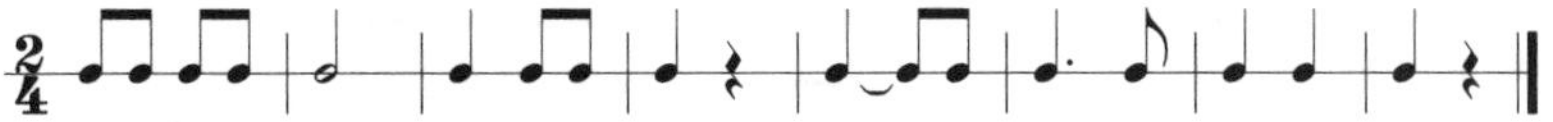

1.20

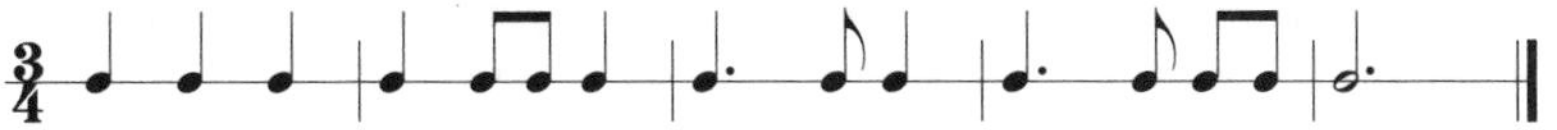

1.21

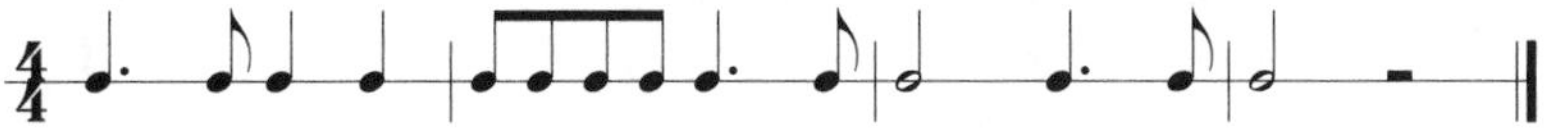

1.22

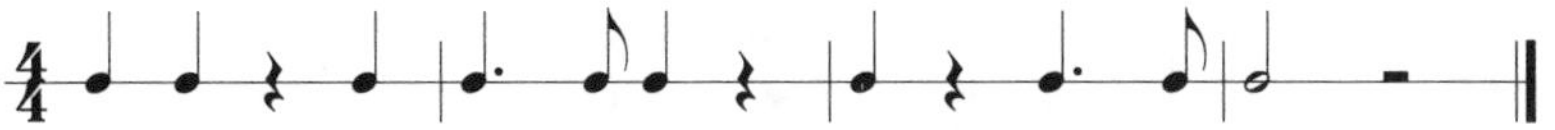

1.23

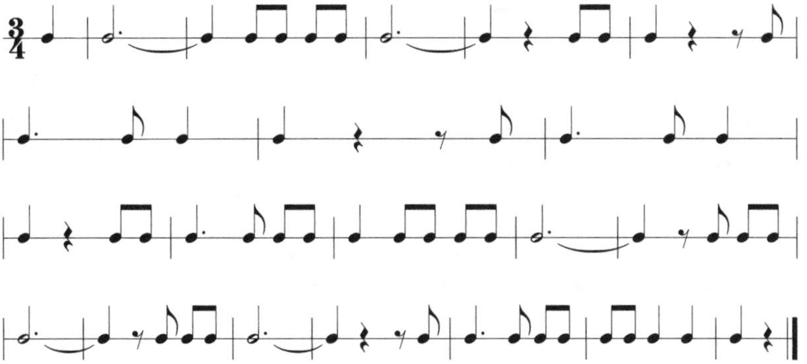

1.24

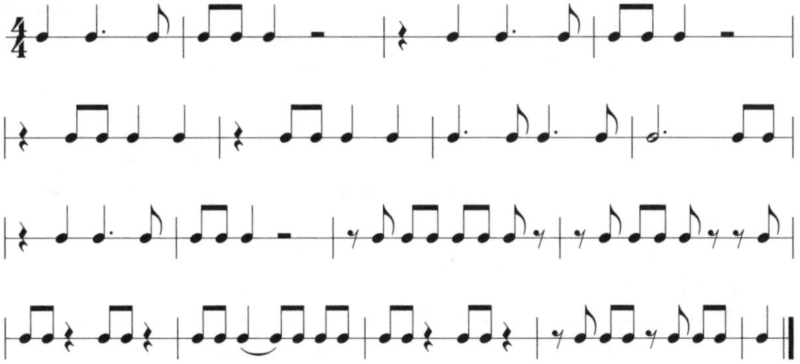

Section 3. Two-part drills.

Suggested methods of performance:

1. One person: Tap both lines, using both hands.
2. One person: Recite one line while tapping the other.
3. Two people: Each recite a line.

Only the meter signatures $\frac{2}{4}$, $\frac{3}{4}$, and $\frac{4}{4}$ will be found in melodies from Section 1 of Chapter 2. Sight-singing studies may begin there at this time.

Section 4. Note values other than the quarter note as beat values.

The half note, the eighth note, and the sixteenth note are also used to represent the beat. The signatures $\frac{2}{2}$ (¢), $\frac{3}{8}$, and $\frac{6}{8}$ are commonly used in written music. Others are occasionally seen. See Chapter 2, Section 3, for melodic examples of less common signatures.

In 1.30, examples *a*, *b*, *c*, and *d* all sound the same when the duration of each of their beat-note values (♩, ♪, ♪, and ♪) is the same.

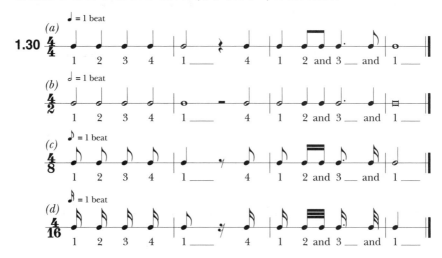

1.31 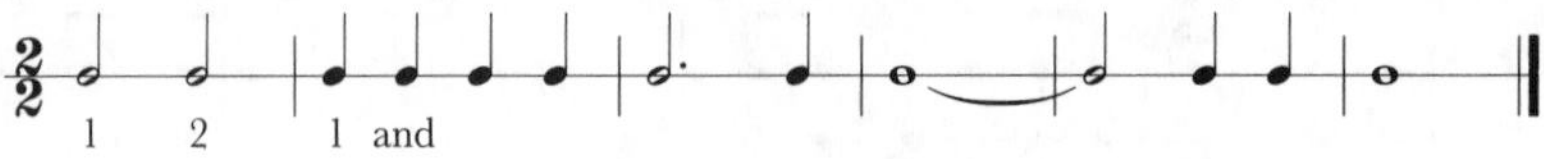

1.32 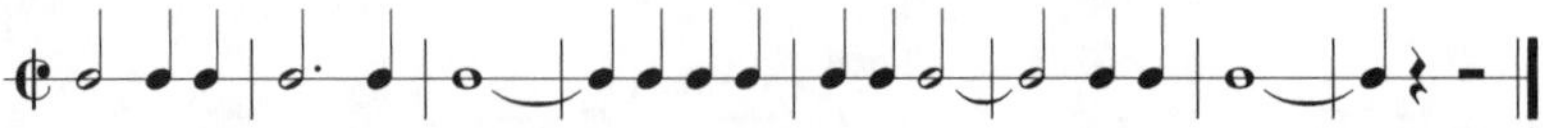

1.33 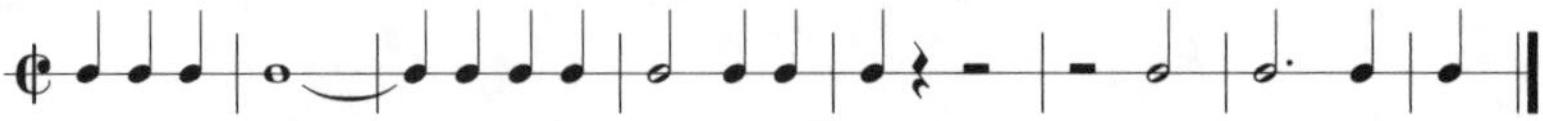

1.34 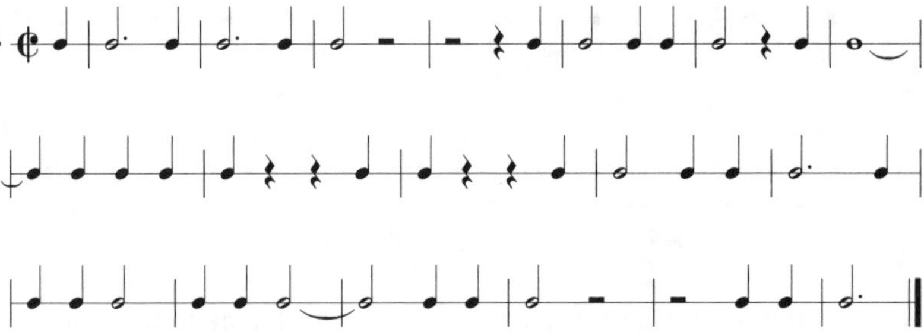

1.35 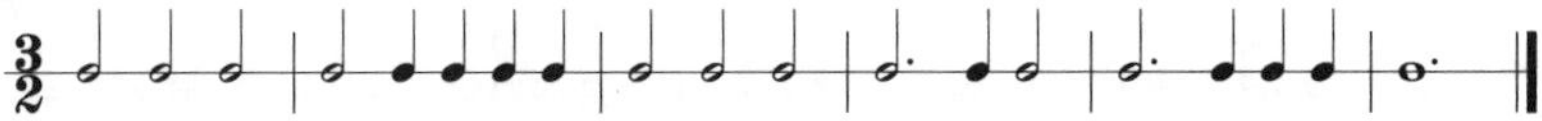

1.36 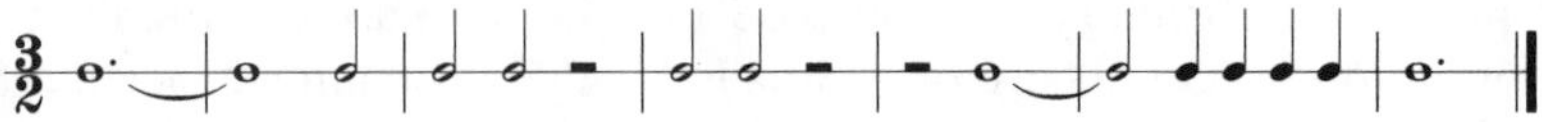

1.37 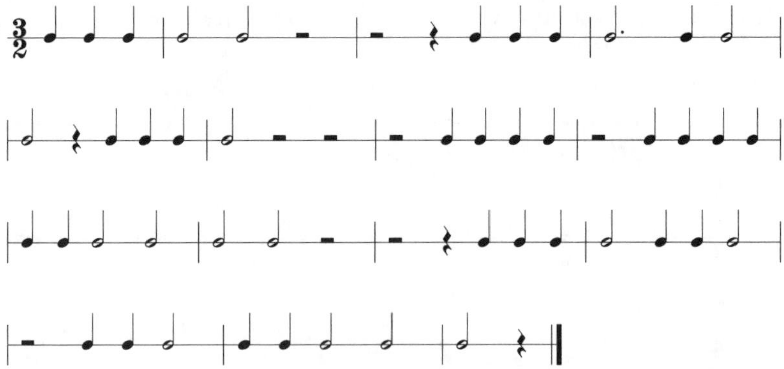

1.38 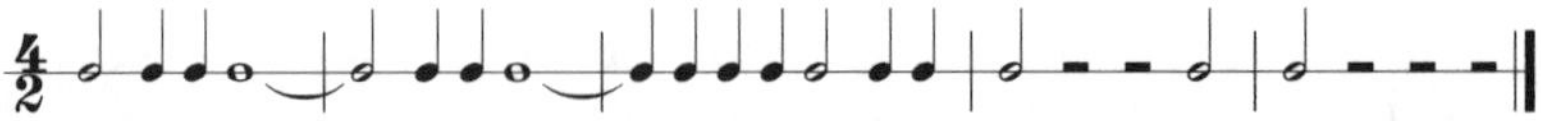

Section 5. Two-part drills.

2

MELODY

stepwise melodies, major keys

RHYTHM

simple meters;
the beat and its division into two parts

SIGHT SINGING

All melodies in Chapter 2 display stepwise movement and in a major key only; each interval is either a whole step (major second) or a half step (minor second).[1] If you can sing a major scale, these melodies should present very little difficulty.

Before reading a given melody, make these general preparations, all of which refer to later chapters in the text as well as to the melodies of this chapter.

1. Look at the key signature. What key does it indicate? On what line or space is the tonic? Does the melody begin on the tonic tone, or on some other pitch? (You may play the tonic note, but no other, immediately before singing.)

2. Scan the melody for passages in stepwise movement and then for larger intervals, particularly those presented in the chapter under study.

3. Observe the phrase marks. The end of a phrase mark usually indicates a cadence (that is, a temporary pause or a final stopping place), much the way commas and periods indicate pauses in language reading. Look ahead to the last note under each phrase mark so that you know where you are heading.

4. Continue the use of the conductor's beat, as described under "Rhythmic Reading" on page 2. Remember that "sight singing" refers only to the *first* time you sing the melody. Sing to the end of the example without stopping,

[1] Melodies in this chapter were written by Robert Ottman. The remainder of the text includes, for the most part, only folk music or music by recognized composers, but examples from these sources occur too infrequently for the purposes of Chapter 2.

no matter how many mistakes you make. Then go back, review the melody, practice the rough spots, and sing the entire melody again.

There are a variety of ways to accomplish sight singing:

1. *Sing solfège syllables.* The tonic note is *do*, followed by the syllables shown below for each scale step.[2] In a major key, the syllables *mi-fa* and *ti-do* always represent half steps. (See Chapter 5 for solfège syllables in minor keys.)

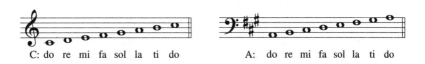

C: do re mi fa sol la ti do   A: do re mi fa sol la ti do

2. *Sing scale-degree numbers.* The tonic note is $\hat{1}$, followed by successive numbers $\hat{2}$ through $\hat{8}$. The carat (^) means "scale-degree," so $\hat{1}$ is simply the first note of the scale. When sung, scale-degree numbers are typically pronounced "one," "two," "three," "four," "five," "six," and "sev" (because the extra syllable in "seven" would change the rhythm—for instance, making a quarter note sound like two eighth notes).

F: $\hat{1}$ $\hat{2}$ $\hat{3}$ $\hat{4}$ $\hat{5}$ $\hat{6}$ $\hat{7}$ $\hat{8}$ (or $\hat{1}$)

3. *Sing letter names.* Sing each pitch using its letter name. However, when reading both pitch and rhythm, do not add the word "sharp" or "flat," because this would change the rhythm. If you want to convey the chromatic inflections monosyllabically, consider an adaptation of the German system, where sharp notes end with *is* and flat notes end with *es*—for instance, G♯ is pronounced *Gis* (sounds like "geese") and G♭ is pronounced *Ges* (sounds like "guess"). The exceptions to this pattern are A♯ ("ace") and A♭ ("ice").

Inflected: A B Cis D E Fis Gis A   Ice Bes C Des Es F G Ice
Uninflected: A B C D E F G A   A B C D E F G A

4. *Sing on a neutral syllable.* With sufficient practice in singing scales and intervals, some students find that singing on a neutral syllable such as *la* suffices.

---

[2] This is known as the moveable-*do* solfège system. In the fixed-*do* solfège system, C is always *do*, D is always *re*, and so forth, regardless of the key. The use of solfège syllables began with the work of Guido d'Arezzo (who lived from approximately 991 until some time after 1033 and wrote one of the most widely read music instruction books of the Middle Ages).

Section I. Major keys, treble clef, the quarter note as the beat unit. Key signatures with no more than three sharps or three flats.

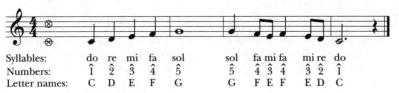

Syllables:	do	re	mi	fa	sol		sol	fa	mi	fa	mi	re	do
Numbers:	$\hat{1}$	$\hat{2}$	$\hat{3}$	$\hat{4}$	$\hat{5}$		$\hat{5}$	$\hat{4}$	$\hat{3}$	$\hat{4}$	$\hat{3}$	$\hat{2}$	$\hat{1}$
Letter names:	C	D	E	F	G		G	F	E	F	E	D	C

⊗ indicates the location of the tonic note.

2.1

2.2

2.3

2.4

2.5

sol
$\hat{5}$

2.6

2.13

2.14

2.15

Melodies occasionally begin on pitches outside of the tonic triad, as in the next two examples. Be sure to identify the key first, then sing a scale from the tonic pitch up or down to the melody's first note. Alternatively, given that the first note necessarily falls within one scale step of $\hat{1}$, $\hat{3}$, or $\hat{5}$, it is also convenient to sing the nearest member of the tonic triad and then move stepwise to the first note of the melody. The latter strategy is depicted here.

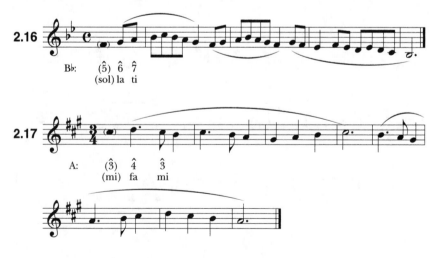

2.16   Bb: ($\hat{5}$) $\hat{6}$ $\hat{7}$
       (sol) la ti

2.17   A: ($\hat{3}$) $\hat{4}$ $\hat{3}$
       (mi) fa mi

Section 2. Bass clef.

Section 3. Other meter signatures.

The meter signatures in melodies 2.32–2.40 are quite common. Review examples in Chapter 1, Section 4.

2.42

2.43

Section 4. Duets.

2.44

2.45

2.46

2.47

2.48

2.49

Section 5. Structured improvisation.

Structured improvisation exercises provide an opportunity to create your own melodies while practicing the skills addressed in each chapter. Sing the notes that are written, and complete the missing portions according to the guidelines provided (indicated by double arrowheads ➤➤ throughout the book). Notice that these exercises, unlike the more traditional rhythms and melodies in the earlier sections of this chapter, may be repeated multiple times because there are many different solutions.[3] (As an example, two distinct answers for exercise 2.50 are illustrated below; numerous other possibilities are left to your imagination.) It is highly recommended that you continue to use your preferred solmization system(s) while improvising.

➤➤ Using entirely stepwise motion, follow the suggested rhythm to fill in the missing notes.

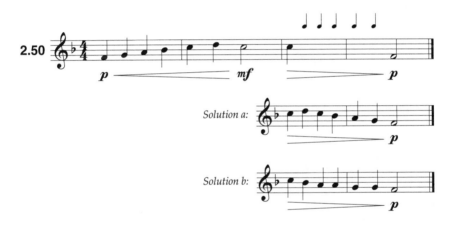

➤➤ Using entirely stepwise motion and no rhythmic value shorter than an eighth note, complete the second phrase.

---

[3] You may even wish to repeat structured improvisation exercises after completing later chapters, in which case you will likely want to incorporate the new material you have learned. For instance, someone returning to the exercises in this chapter after finishing Chapter 3 might prefer to include some leaps from the tonic triad rather than using stepwise motion throughout.

➤➤ Choose a major key and a common simple meter. Using entirely step-wise motion and no rhythmic values shorter than the beat, improvise two four-measure phrases according to the following plan:

- Phrase #1 begins on $\hat{1}$, $\hat{3}$, or $\hat{5}$ and ends on the downbeat of measure 4 on $\hat{2}$.
- Phrase #2 ends on the downbeat of measure 8 on $\hat{1}$.

2.52

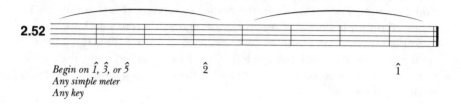

Begin on $\hat{1}$, $\hat{3}$, or $\hat{5}$ $\hat{2}$ $\hat{1}$
Any simple meter
Any key

Variation: work with a partner so that one person sings the first phrase and the other person sings the second phrase. Then try again with the roles reversed.

3

MELODY

intervals from the tonic triad, major keys

RHYTHM

simple meters

The melodies of this chapter contain several intervals larger than the scale steps of Chapter 2. Singing these particular intervals will be easy, since all are included in the tonic triad. If you can recognize and sing the three members of the tonic triad, you should have little or no problem when they occur in the melodies of this chapter.

In C major, the tonic triad is C E G; the possible intervals between any two of these pitches are as follows:[1]

        M3rd   m3rd   P5th   P4th   m6th   M6th   P8ve

M = major, m = minor, P = perfect

The members of the C-major triad at *a* in the following exercise are arranged melodically at *b* and *c*. Sing these on scale-degree numbers or solfège syllables.[1]

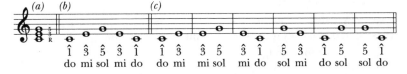

      (a) *(b)*   *(c)*

        $\hat{1}$ $\hat{3}$ $\hat{5}$ $\hat{3}$ $\hat{1}$ $\hat{1}$ $\hat{3}$ $\hat{3}$ $\hat{5}$ $\hat{3}$ $\hat{1}$ $\hat{5}$ $\hat{3}$ $\hat{1}$ $\hat{5}$ $\hat{5}$ $\hat{1}$
        do mi sol mi do   do mi   mi sol   mi do   sol mi   do sol   sol do

[1] "R," "3," and "5" refer here to a triad's root, third, and fifth, respectively. In this chapter, these chord members coincide with $\hat{1}$, $\hat{3}$, and $\hat{5}$—that is, the first, third, and fifth scale degrees. See page 80 for an example of a nontonic triad.

Now add higher notes, lower notes, or both from the C-major triad, and sing the new available intervals.

$\hat{5}$ $\hat{1}$ $\hat{3}$ $\hat{1}$ $\hat{5}$ $\hat{3}$ $\hat{5}$ $\hat{3}$ $\hat{1}$ $\hat{5}$ $\hat{1}$ $\hat{3}$ $\hat{3}$ $\hat{5}$ $\hat{3}$ $\hat{5}$

sol do   mi do   sol mi   sol mi   do sol   do mi   mi sol   mi sol

Here are successions of several intervals from the tonic triad, first in C major, then in several other keys. For each key, first sing $\hat{1}$-$\hat{3}$-$\hat{5}$-$\hat{3}$-$\hat{1}$, *do-mi-sol-mi-do*, or letter names, carefully noting the location of each of these on the staff. You can see that if $\hat{1}$ (*do*) is on a line, $\hat{3}$ (*mi*) and $\hat{5}$ (*sol*) are on the next two lines above; or if $\hat{1}$ is on a space, $\hat{3}$ and $\hat{5}$ are on the two spaces above.

Pay particular attention to the unique sound of each of these intervals from the tonic triad. Memorize these sounds as soon as possible. These intervals are frequently used in other melodic or harmonic configurations.

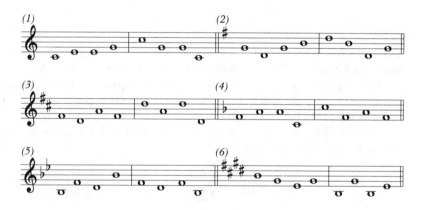

Now we are ready to sing melodies that include both stepwise motion and intervals from the given melody's tonic triad. Follow these steps in preparation for singing each melody:

1. Determine the key.
2. Spell the tonic triad.
3. Locate the tonic triad on the staff.
4. Scan the melody for examples of intervals in the tonic triad.
5. Sing the tonic triad.

Try this procedure on the following melody:

Note that:

1. The key is E♭ major.
2. The tonic triad is spelled E♭ G B♭.
3. The tonic triad is located on the first, second, and third lines. Also locate higher and lower tones of the triad on the staff.

4. Find intervals that are members of this triad.
5. Sing these intervals.

Section 1. Major keys, treble clef, intervals of the third, fourth, fifth, and octave from the tonic triad. The quarter note as the beat unit. Key signatures in this chapter are limited to four sharps or flats until Section 6.

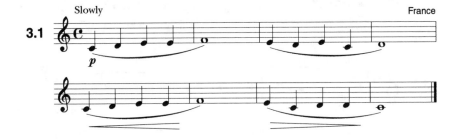

*♪ is a "grace note," to be sung as quickly as possible.

² Review the text preceding melody number 2.16.

³ This melody is from a collection in which Brahms set folk songs as vocal solos with piano accompaniment. Others will be found on later pages of this text.

Canon for 3 voices

P. Hayes (18th century)

Section 2. Bass clef.

Slowly

France

Allegro assai

Mozart, Serenade, K. 237

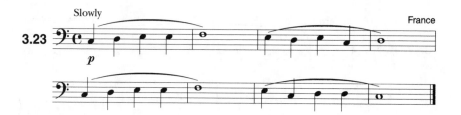

Allegretto

Germany

Allegro

Germany

3.27 Allegro — Fr. Silcher (1842), *Alle Jahre wieder*

3.28 Allegretto — Spain

3.29 Allegro — Handel, *Judas Maccabaeus*

3.30 Schubert, Waltz, D. 146, No. 8

3.31 Moderato — Spain

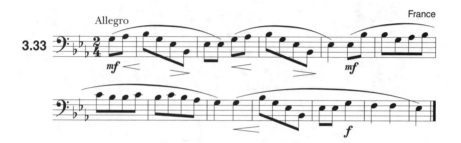

Section 3. Interval of the sixth: minor sixth, $\hat{3}$ up to $\hat{1}$, and major sixth, $\hat{5}$ up to $\hat{3}$, or descending.

34

3.40 Moderato — Ohio

3.41 Canon for 4 voices — Beethoven

3.42 Canon for 3 voices — England

3.43 Canon for 4 voices — P. Hayes

Section 4. The half note and the eighth note as beat units.

3.44 Andante — Slovakia

37

Section 5. Duets.

The asterisk (*) indicates the original folk song, to which a second line has been added.

3.52 Andante .... Germany

Andante con moto .... Germany

3.53

3.54 Allegro Germany

3.55 France

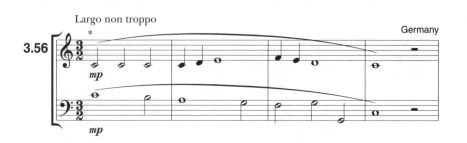

3.56 Largo non troppo Germany

40

Section 6. Key signatures with five, six, and seven sharps or flats.

Although these key signatures are not used as frequently as the easier signatures, their use from the eighteenth century to the present is significant enough to warrant your attention. Bach used them in the two volumes of his *Well-Tempered Clavier* to demonstrate that any note of the chromatic scale could be used as a tonic. They were especially favored in the music of nineteenth-century Romantic composers such as Chopin, Brahms, Liszt, and Wagner.

If you find these key signatures intimidating, note that for the scale of every "difficult" signature, there is an "easy" scale using the identical lines and spaces of the staff. Shown here are the first five notes of the G♭-major scale (key signature, six flats) and G-major scale (key signature, one sharp). The two *look* alike on paper, so if you can read these notes in G major, G♭ major should be just as easy.

Here are the "difficult" keys, each with an "easy" key for which the staff notation is identical. When sight singing, cover the given key signature and think its easy counterpart. Then sing again, in the given key.

5♯, B major	.2♭, B♭ major	5♭, D♭ major	.2♯, D major
6♯, F♯ major	.1♭, F major	6♭, G♭ major	.1♯, G major
7♯, C♯ major	.0, C major	7♭, C♭ major	.0, C major

With the introduction of accidentals in later chapters, it can be cumbersome to use this procedure, so be sure you can now spell the scales of these keys quickly and easily. Then practice while the melodies are still easy, rather than working with them for the first time when the melodies are more difficult.

3.60 Allegro — Silesia
mf (repeat *p*)
mf

3.61 Moderato — Silesia
mp
mf
p   *rit.*   *pp*

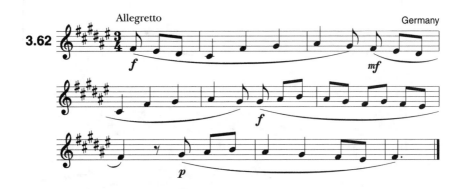

3.62 Allegretto — Germany
f   *mf*
f
p

3.63 Allegretto — Spain
p
pp

43

Section 7. Structured improvisation.

➤➤ Complete the two phrases using only notes from the tonic triad. A suitable rhythm has been indicated.

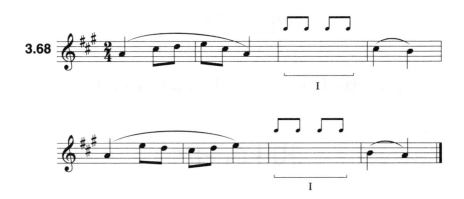

3.68

➤➤ Using only notes from the tonic triad, follow the suggested rhythm to complete the phrase.

3.69

➤➤ Following the given rhythm, use stepwise motion and leaps from the tonic triad (as indicated below each bracket) to complete the two phrases.

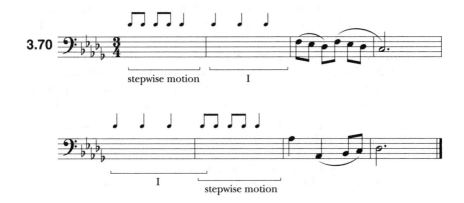

3.70

4

MELODY

intervals from the tonic triad, major keys

RHYTHM

compound meters;
the beat and its division into three parts

The melodies of this chapter include only those intervals already presented in Chapter 3. New to this chapter is the use of compound meter.

In compound meter, the beat is divisible into three parts, and therefore it can be represented only by a dotted note value. In a $\frac{6}{8}$ meter, for example, the dotted quarter note representing the beat is divisible into three eighth notes ($\quarternote\!. = \eighthnote\eighthnote\eighthnote$). Two dotted quarter notes, therefore, equal six eighth notes; hence the signature $\frac{6}{8}$ ($2 \times \frac{3}{8} = \frac{6}{8}$).

Compound meter signatures show 6, 9, and 12 in the numerator but are ordinarily conducted as two, three, and four beats, respectively, each with three pulses per beat. A simpler compound meter signature exists but, unfortunately, is little used. Instead of $\frac{6}{8}$, for example, the signature $\frac{2}{\quarternote\!.}$ is an exact description of the meter: two beats per measure and a dotted quarter note receives one beat. Some similar meter signatures are $\frac{3}{\quarternote\!.}$ instead of $\frac{9}{8}$, $\frac{4}{\quarternote\!.}$ instead of $\frac{12}{8}$, and so forth.

There are a variety of good rhythmic syllable systems to reflect compound meters. Your choice of syllables in compound meters will, of course, be influenced by your choice of syllables in simple meters. Several popular systems are illustrated below, or you may wish to use another approach.

   a. Any note falling on a beat is given one syllable (such as *du*), and notes falling on the divisions of the beat are given their own syllables (such as *da di*, pronounced "dah dee").
   b. Any note falling on a beat is named by the beat number, and notes falling on the divisions of the beat are given their own syllables (often *la lee*).

c. Any note falling on a beat is named by the beat number, and all other notes are given the same neutral syllable (such as *ta*).

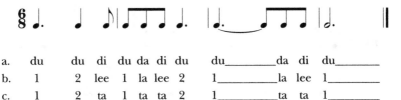

a.	du		du	di	du	da	di	du	du_____	da	di	du_____
b.	1		2	lee	1	la	lee	2	1_____	la	lee	1_____
c.	1		2	ta	1	ta	ta	2	1_____	ta	ta	1_____

Melodies in compound meters are far less common than those in simple meters. Of the possible meter signatures, those with a numerator of 6 are the most frequently used. Sections 1 and 4, "Rhythmic Reading," in this chapter will include a variety of compound meter signatures. Melodies at the level of this chapter in compound triple and compound quadruple meters are virtually nonexistent in music literature. Melodies 2.51–2.54, written by Robert Ottman, use selected meter signatures to provide introductory practice.

Section 1. Rhythmic reading: The dotted quarter note as the beat unit. Single lines and two-part drills.

4.18
4.19
4.20
4.21
4.22

4.23

Section 2. Sight singing: major keys, treble clef; the dotted quarter note as the beat unit.

4.24   Allegro   Russia

4.25   Allegro   England

4.26   Allegretto   England

4.27   Deciso   Germany

4.28   Vif   France

4.29   Moderato   England

4.30   Allegro moderato   England

4.31   Lively   France

4.32 Canada

Fine

D.C. al Fine

4.33 Lightly — England

4.34 Con moto — England

mf

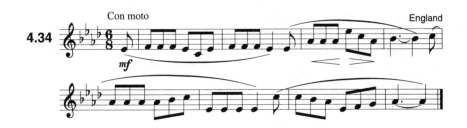

4.35 Allegro vivo — Tchaikovsky, *The Queen of Spades*, Op. 68

f

4.36 Con spirito — England

4.37 Con moto — United States

Section 3. Sight singing: Bass clef.

4.38 Rather slow — France

4.39 Allegretto — England

54

4.49 Allegretto   England

4.50 Moderato   England

4.51

4.52

4.53

57

Section 4. Rhythmic reading: The dotted half note and the dotted eighth note as beat units, including two-part drills.

In number 4.55, examples *a, b,* and *c* sound the same when the duration of their respective beat notes (♩., ♩., ♪.) is the same.

Section 5. Sight singing: The dotted half note and dotted eighth note as beat units.

Section 6. Duets.

Section 7. Structured improvisation.

➤➤ Use stepwise motion and leaps from the tonic triad (as shown below each bracket) to complete the phrase. A rhythm has been indicated for measure 2, but you should improvise your own rhythm for measure 4.

➤➤ In measure 1, notes have been provided, but you will need to improvise your own rhythm. Use any combination of ♪, ♩, and ♩. that fits the meter. In measure 3, use only notes from the tonic triad, improvising your own rhythm.

➤➤ Complete the melody with notes from the tonic triad, using any combination of ♪, ♩, and ♩. that fits the meter.

5

MELODY

minor keys;
intervals from the tonic triad

RHYTHM

simple and compound meters

In minor keys, most melodic lines conform to the melodic form of the minor scale, using ↑6̂ and ↑7̂ (raised 6̂ and raised 7̂) ascending and ↓6̂ and ↓7̂ (natural 6̂ and natural 7̂) descending.[1] In the traditional use of syllables, the tonic tone is designated *la*, ensuring that *mi-fa* and *ti-do* are half steps and all other adjacent syllables are whole steps. The chromatic tones ↑6̂ and ↑7̂ require the syllables *fi* and *si* from the chromatic scale, while ↓7̂ and ↓6̂ use the normal *sol* and *fa*, as shown below.

In modern practice, there is a growing preference for designating the tonic as *do* in minor keys, also shown below. An advantage is the consistent use of *do* for tonic. Lost in this system is the original concept that half steps in either mode should always be identified as *mi-fa* or *ti-do*.

When singing with numbers, generally avoid singing "sharp" or "flat" with 6̂ and 7̂ to lessen the number of syllables on a single note.

C minor

	1̂	2̂	3̂	4̂	5̂	↑6̂	↑7̂	8̂		8̂	↓7̂	↓6̂	5̂	4̂	3̂	2̂	1̂
Traditional:	la	ti	do	re	mi	fi	si	la		la	sol	fa	mi	re	do	ti	la
Modern:	do	re	me	fa	sol	la	ti	do		do	te	le	sol	fa	me	re	do

[1] When a melodic line contains an ascending ↓7̂, or ↑6̂ without an accompanying ↑7̂, that line is often based on one of the diatonic modes. See Chapter 20.

Follow these steps as preparation for sight singing in a minor key:

1. Be sure you can accurately sing the complete melodic minor scale in the key of the melody, both ascending and descending. Practice with letter names and with either numbers or syllables.

2. Look for examples of ↓$\hat{6}$ and ↓$\hat{7}$ and of ↑$\hat{6}$ and ↑$\hat{7}$.

G minor   ↓$\hat{7}$ ↓$\hat{6}$ ↓$\hat{6}$ ↑$\hat{6}$ ↑$\hat{7}$ ↑$\hat{7}$

3. Note special uses of $\hat{6}$ and $\hat{7}$.

   a. In the succession $\hat{6}$–$\hat{7}$–$\hat{6}$, the direction of the last tone of this group determines which form of the scale is used for all three notes. See melody 5.3, measure 2. In the group B♭–C–B♭ ($\hat{6}$–$\hat{7}$–$\hat{6}$ in D minor), the final B♭ descends; therefore, all three notes are from the descending form of the scale.

   b. In the succession ↑$\hat{7}$–↑$\hat{6}$–↑$\hat{7}$, the direction of the last tone of this group determines that the ascending form of the scale is used for all three notes. See melody 5.3, measure 3. In the group C♯–B–C♯ (↑$\hat{7}$–↑$\hat{6}$–↑$\hat{7}$ in D minor), the final C♯ ascends; therefore, all three notes are from the ascending form of the scale.

   c. The descending succession ↑$\hat{7}$–↑$\hat{6}$ implies the use of dominant harmony at that point. In melody 5.7, the descending scale line A–G–F♯–E♮–D in G minor implies a V triad, A–F♯–D, with a passing tone between A and F♯ and between F♯ and D.

4. Recognize intervals. The same intervals used to construct a major triad are used to construct a minor triad. The perfect intervals (P4, P5, and P8) remain the same, but the major and minor intervals are reversed:

	Major Triad	*Minor Triad*
R up to 3	M3	m3
3 up to 5	m3	M3
3 up to R	m6	M6
5 up to 3	M6	m6
R up to 5	P5	P5
5 up to R	P4	P4

All intervals from the D-minor triad are here arranged melodically. Sing these on scale-degree numbers or solfège syllables.

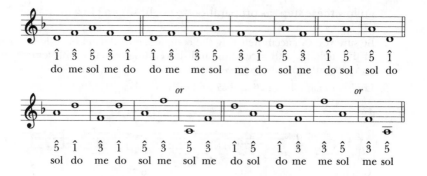

$\hat{1}$ $\hat{3}$ $\hat{5}$ $\hat{3}$ $\hat{1}$ $\hat{1}$ $\hat{3}$ $\hat{3}$ $\hat{5}$ $\hat{3}$ $\hat{1}$ $\hat{5}$ $\hat{3}$ $\hat{1}$ $\hat{5}$ $\hat{5}$ $\hat{1}$

do me sol me do   do me   me sol   me do   sol me   do sol   sol do

or   *or*

$\hat{5}$ $\hat{1}$ $\hat{3}$ $\hat{1}$ $\hat{5}$ $\hat{3}$ $\hat{5}$ $\hat{3}$ $\hat{1}$ $\hat{5}$ $\hat{1}$ $\hat{3}$ $\hat{3}$ $\hat{5}$ $\hat{3}$ $\hat{5}$

sol do   me do   sol me   sol me   do sol   do me   me sol   me sol

Here are successions of intervals from the tonic triad in various minor keys. Sing each group with numbers or with syllables.

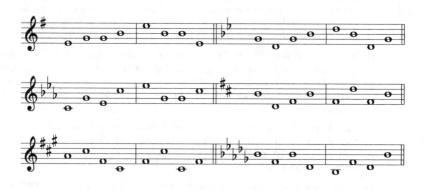

Section I. Simple meters.

5.1 $\uparrow\hat{7}$ $\downarrow\hat{7}$ $\downarrow\hat{6}$ $\downarrow\hat{7}$ $\uparrow\hat{6}$ $\uparrow\hat{7}$

do ti do re   do te le sol   fa sol le sol la ti do

5.2

5.3 $\downarrow\hat{6}\downarrow\hat{7}\downarrow\hat{6}$ $\uparrow\hat{7}$ $\uparrow\hat{6}\uparrow\hat{7}$

5.4

5.7   i   V (D F♯ A)   i   V   i

Canon for 4 voices

Haydn

Schubert, *Ecossaises,* D. 145, No. 1

5.12

Lent

France

5.13

Canon for 4 voices

England

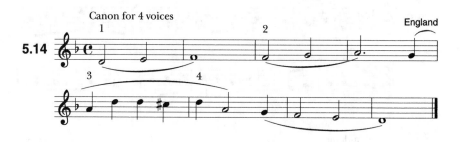

5.14

Adagio

England

5.15

5.25 Non troppo lento — Portugal

Section 2. Compound meters.

5.26 Andante — Basque — *Fine* — *D.C.*

5.27 Andante — Wales

5.28 Allegretto — Wales

Section 3. Duets.

5.37 Triste et lent

France

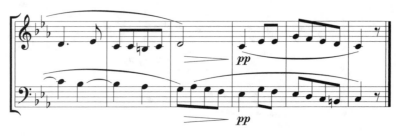

5.38 Adagio

France

5.39 Moderato

Slovakia

France

5.40 Vif

Section 4. Structured improvisation.

▶▶ Complete this melody using stepwise motion and maintaining a constant eighth-note pattern until the last note. To help shape the melody, the first eighth note of every group (that is, the eighth note that falls on each beat) has been provided.

▶▶ Use stepwise motion and leaps from the tonic triad (as shown below each bracket) to complete the melody. A rhythm has been suggested.

➤➤ Improvise a second phrase using stepwise motion and leaps from the tonic triad. Restrict yourself to rhythmic values no shorter than an eighth note. As indicated, you should end with the tonic on the downbeat of measure 8.

5.44

6

MELODY

intervals from the dominant (V) triad;
major and minor keys

RHYTHM

simple and compound meters

Intervals from the dominant triad, very common in melodic writing, are the same as those from the tonic triad, but in a different context. In major keys, syllable names for members of the V triad are *sol–ti–re* (ascending), and the scale-degree numbers are $\hat{5}$–$\hat{7}$–$\hat{2}$, as at *a* and *b* below. Observe also that at *c*, its members can be identified as R–3–5 *of the triad*.

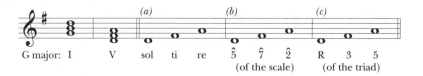

In minor keys, the dominant triad has the same sound as in major keys, since the leading tone is the *raised seventh* scale degree ($\uparrow\hat{7}$).

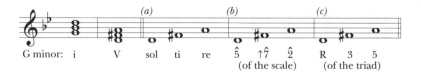

Observe these characteristics of the various possible intervals:

1. Skips to the third of the triad (the *leading tone*) are easy, since the second note of the interval, no matter what the size of the interval, is always a half step below the tonic.

2. Skips to the root of the triad are easy because this root is $\hat{5}$ *(the dominant)* of the scale.

3. Skips to the fifth of the triad are skips to the tone above the tonic *(supertonic)*.

Any skip in the dominant triad will be either to the dominant tone or to a scale step above or below the tonic tone, so remembering the sound of the tonic and dominant tones of the key (as learned in Chapters 3–5) is important.

Before singing, spell the tonic and dominant triads. Then scan the melody for location of intervals from the dominant triad. Example:

Observe that:

1. The key is G major. I = G B D.
2. The dominant (V) triad is D F♯ A.
3. At *a* (interval, D down to A), the leap is to $\hat{2}$, the scale step above the tonic.
4. At *b*, the intervals outline the V triad.
5. At *c*, the interval, though large, is simply a skip to the leading tone, the scale step below the tonic.

Section 1. Intervals of the third from the V triad; major keys; simple meters.

6.10 Lustily — Germany — **f**

6.11 Allegretto — Louisiana — **mp** — 1. 2.

6.12 Moderato — Germany — **mf** — cresc. — **f**

Section 2. Intervals of the third from the V triad; minor keys; simple meters.

6.13 Allegro risoluto — Netherlands — **f**

6.14 Largo — Sweden — **p** — **mf** — **pp**

6.15 Fast — England

6.16 Moderato — Germany

Mozart, *The Abduction from the Seraglio*, K. 384

6.17 Allegro assai

Section 3. Intervals of the fourth and fifth from the V triad; major and minor keys; simple meters.

6.22 Schubert, Minuet

6.23 Allegro spirito — France

6.24 Con moto — Germany

6.25 Allegretto — Poland

6.26 Allegro — Austria

Canon for 2 voices

Wachsmann (1791–1853)

6.31

Canon for 3 voices

England

6.32

My dame has in her hutch at home a lit - tle dog,

Hey, dog, hey with a clog.

Ziemlich schnell

Schubert, *Erstarrung,* Op. 89, No. 4

6.33

p

Andante

Beranger, *Ce jour-là*

6.34

p

Ruhig

Germany

6.35

pp   *mp*   *p*

pp

Section 4. Interval of the sixth from the V triad; simple meters.

Section 5. Compound meters; various intervals from the V triad.

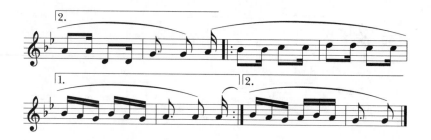

Section 6. Numerator of 3, compound meters.

Melodies with a numerator of 3 in the meter signature and with fast tempo indications are very often performed with a single beat per measure. The effect is that of compound meter, one beat per measure, as shown in the next four examples.

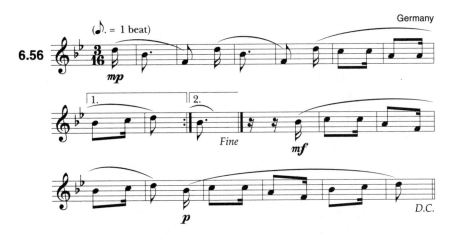

6.56 Germany

6.57 Canada

Section 7. Duets.

6.58 Germany

6.59 Lebhaft

Austria

6.60 Allegretto

Canada

6.61 Lentement   France

6.62 Allegro con brio   Netherlands

6.63 Allegretto   Sweden

97

6.64

Andante

Netherlands

Section 8. Structured improvisation.

➤➤ Complete this melody using notes from the dominant triad. Suitable rhythms have been suggested in most places, but you will need to improvise your own rhythm in measure 7 (restrict yourself to rhythmic values no shorter than an eighth note).

➤➤ Complete this melody using notes from the tonic and dominant triads (as indicated below each bracket). A suitable rhythm has been suggested.

➤➤ Complete this melody using notes from the tonic and dominant triads (as indicated below each bracket). A suitable rhythm has been suggested.

7

THE C CLEFS

alto and tenor clefs

The clef sign 𝄡, or less commonly 𝕂, indicates the location of *middle C* on the staff. When found on the third line of the staff, the C clef is known as the "alto clef," and when found on the fourth line, it is known as the "tenor clef."

alto clef · tenor clef

The alto clef is commonly used by the viola, the tenor clef by the cello, the trombone, and the bassoon, and each occasionally by other instruments. The ability to read music in these clefs is important, not only to the players of these instruments, but also to any musician studying orchestral scores such as those for symphonies, or chamber music scores such as those for string quartets. Those studying music written before about 1700, either in original scores or in modern musicological editions, will find that these two C clefs, together with the soprano clef, the mezzo soprano clef, and the baritone clef (indicating F), are used freely in vocal and instrumental music.

soprano clef · mezzo soprano clef · baritone clef

Section I. The alto clef.

Before attempting to sing at sight in any C clef, be sure to learn the names of the lines and spaces in that clef, just as you did when learning to read the treble and bass clefs. These are the names of the lines and spaces in the alto clef:

F G A B C D E F G   F A C E G   G B D F

All of the melodies in this chapter use only those melodic and rhythmic materials already presented in previous chapters. To facilitate fluent clef reading, try singing melodies using the correct letter names. When singing in letter names, you may omit the words "sharp" and "flat" or use the German system to avoid changing the melody's rhythm (see page 13). The melody *America* is written in alto and bass clef (melodies 7.1*a* and 7.1*b*); although the notation differs, the pitches are identical.

7.17 Andante con moto — Germany

7.18 Andante — England

7.19 Lento — England

Section 2. The tenor clef.

These are the names of the lines and spaces of the tenor clef:

D E F G A B C D E   D F A C E   E G B D

Also note that in the tenor clef, the first sharp of the key signature is on the second line, with the following sharps in the pattern fifth up and fourth down. This arrangement avoids the use of ledger lines.

After learning the names of the lines and spaces, sing with letter names the tune *America* as shown in melody 7.20. Its sound is identical to that of *America* in melodies 7.1*a* and 7.1*b*.

America

7.20

G G A F(♯) G A B B C B A G A G F(♯) G
       Fis   Fis

Maestoso

Germany

7.21

Allegretto

England

7.22

Canon for 4 voices

Brahms

7.28

Andantino

Germany

7.29

Canon for 4 voices

Praetorius

7.30

England

7.31

Section 3. Additional practice in the C clefs.

Any melody in the treble or bass clef can be used for sight singing in either of the C clefs. We will again use *America* to demonstrate.

G G A F(♯) G A B B C B A G
          Fis

1. Locate the line or the space of the tonic note. In *America* above, the tonic note is on the second line.

2. Ignore the given treble or bass clef, and imagine in its place an alto clef. With the alto clef, the second line is still tonic. Since the second line is A, the tonic is now A (or A♭). Add the appropriate key signature and sing the letter names in the key of A (A♭).

A A B G(♯) A B C(♯) C(♯) D C(♯) B A
          Gis   Cis Cis   Cis

3. In the tenor clef, the second line is F (or F♯). Proceed as above. The key will be F (or F♯). Sing the letter names in this key.

F F G E F G A A B(♭) A G F
                        Bes

8

MELODY

further use of diatonic intervals

RHYTHM

simple and compound meters

Melodies from previous chapters have included the intervals most frequently used in melodic writing: major and minor seconds, major and minor thirds, major and minor sixths, the perfect fourth, and the perfect fifth. Intervals larger than the second were learned as used in tonic and dominant triads, contexts very frequently used and easy to read. This chapter presents the same intervals in different contexts.

For students correlating sight singing and harmonic studies, recognizing the particular use of an interval helps to achieve success in both areas. Here are new contexts you should be looking for.

1. Two successive intervals may outline a triad other than tonic or dominant. The subdominant and supertonic triads are those most frequently found in melodic form, as in melody 8.1 (IV triad) and melody 8.4 (ii triad). Look for the use of a different complete triad in melody 8.27.

2. Commonly, an interval may not imply a single harmony, even though the two tones of the interval may be members of some triad. As an example, look at melody 8.40.

   Measures 1–2: C up to F *looks* like the fifth up to the root of the V triad, and F down to B♭ *looks* like the fifth down to the root of the I triad. In each interval, the two tones are members of different triads.

   Measures 9–10: B♭ up to D *looks* like the root up to the third of the I triad, and A up to C *looks* like the third up to the fifth of the V triad. In each interval, the second tone actually functions as a nonharmonic tone, an appoggiatura in this case.

measures 1–2

I   ii   V   I

measures 9–10

app.   app.

I   ii   V   I

When the measures above are combined with measures 5–6, as heard when the canon is performed, the harmonic context is complete and the functions of the intervals can be clearly seen and heard.

app.   app.

I   ii   V   I

3. Frequently you will encounter the easy minor third $\hat{2}$ up to $\hat{4}$ or $\hat{4}$ down to $\hat{2}$. Most often, this interval implies not the ii triad but the fifth and seventh of the V^7 chord, to be presented in Chapter 9. This interval is commonly found in melodies more difficult than those of the previous chapters.

Suggestion: before singing, scan the melody to locate examples of any of the foregoing uses of diatonic intervals.

Section I. Single-line melodies.

Allegro   Pomerania

8.1 f

Allegro   Germany

8.2 f

112

8.6   Con moto   Germany

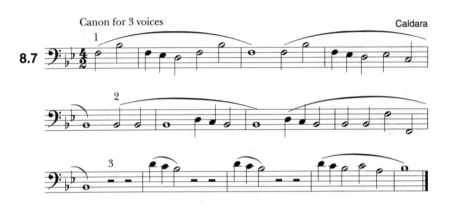

8.7   Canon for 3 voices   Caldara

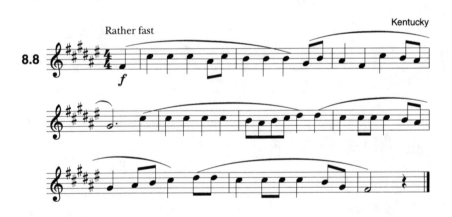

8.8   Rather fast   Kentucky

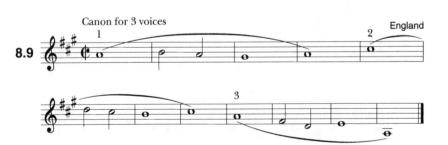

8.9   Canon for 3 voices   England

What triad is outlined by the first three notes of melody 8.10?

8.14

Andante con moto

Mendelssohn, *Das Schifflein*, Op. 99, No. 4

8.15

Andante con moto

Spain

Fine

D.C. al Fine

8.16

Adagio

Canada

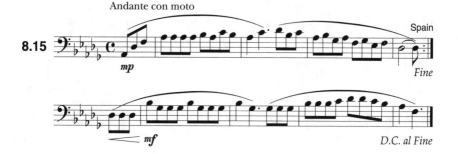

8.17

Canon for 3 voices

Schubert

Canon for 4 voices — Germany

Pas trop lent — France

Andante — Denmark

Before performing melody 8.21, review the text preceding melody 6.54, page 94.

8.21 Allegro (♩. = 1 beat)   Mozart, Divertimento No. 2, K. 131

8.22 Canon for 3 voices (♩. = 1 beat)   Anonymous

8.23 Canon for 3 voices   England

8.29 Allegro — Mozart, Symphony No. 10, K. 74

8.30 Allegretto — Argentina

8.31 Andante — Netherlands

8.32 Lively — Ireland

8.33 Molto moderato — Spain

Canon for 3 voices — Germany

8.37

Canon for 4 voices — Haydn

8.38

Canon for 3 voices — Praetorius

8.39

Canon for 3 voices — Mozart

8.40

8.41 Andante sostenuto — Massenet, *Chant Provençal*

p *dolce* *poco rit.*

8.42 Andante — Germany

mp

8.43 Moderato — Schubert, *Der Entfernten*

mf

8.44 Moderato — England

mf

8.45 Allegretto — Poland
mf *f* *sfz* *cresc.*

Canon for 3 voices — England

8.46

Canon for 4 voices — Germany

8.47

Section 2. Duets.

8.51

Andantino Latvia

8.52

Largo Handel, *Ahi, nelle sorti*

8.53

Chédeville, *Duo Galante VI*

Mozart, String Quartet, K. 458
(Orig: B♭)

Allegro vivace assai

8.54

Section 3. Structured improvisation.

Up until this point, you have been asked to outline specific triads simply by using their chord members exclusively (for instance, singing only $\hat{1}$, $\hat{3}$, and $\hat{5}$ for the tonic triad). However, it is possible—and, indeed, very typical—to convey a triad unambiguously even when notes outside the triad are also included. Stepwise motion between chord members is common, particularly when the chord members are emphasized through their metrical placement.

As an illustration, three different elaborations of the tonic triad and one elaboration of the dominant triad are shown below.

As you will quickly realize, the number of distinct possibilities is virtually unlimited. The additional notes are frequently described as *passing* (if they connect two different chord members by step) or *neighboring* (if they connect two identical notes by step).

▶▶ Complete the next two melodies by singing elaborations of the triad indicated below each bracket. Suitable rhythms have been suggested.

▶▶ Create your own melody by improvising elaborations of the tonic, subdominant, and dominant triads (as indicated below each bracket). Use any combination of ♪, ♩, and ♩. that fits the meter, being sure to end with a suitably conclusive rhythm. (Helpful hint: before you begin, sing a simple arpeggiation of the underlying I–IV–V–I progression.)

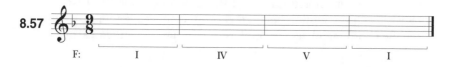

9

MELODY

intervals from the
dominant seventh chord (V⁷);
other diatonic intervals of the seventh

RHYTHM

simple and compound meters

The dominant seventh chord is a four-note chord, the dominant triad plus an additional minor seventh above its root. Of all the possible intervals from this chord, these have not previously been presented:

Root up to seventh or seventh down to root = minor seventh (m7)

Third up to seventh or seventh down to third = diminished fifth (d5), or tritone[1]

Seventh up to third or third down to seventh = augmented fourth (A4), or tritone

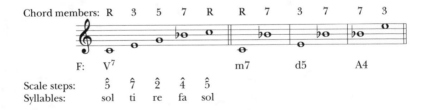

[1] The term *tritone* refers to an interval composed of three whole steps—technically an A4. Because the d5 is enharmonic with the A4, it is also frequently described as a tritone.

Section I. The complete dominant seventh chord.

In this section, successive chord tones outline a complete four-note V^7 chord or the near-complete V^7 chord (chord members R–5–7 or reverse), all utilizing only the intervals of the major third, the minor third, and the perfect fifth.

9.5 Allegro moderato — Canada

9.6 Andante ♩. = 58 — Fauré, *Les Berceaux*

9.7 Allegro — Germany

Section 2. The interval of the minor seventh: $\hat{5}$ up to $\hat{4}$ or reverse.

9.8 Moderato — Memel

9.13 Andante · · · Germany · · · *p* · · · *mp* · · · *p* · · · *pp*

9.14 Haydn, Divertimento · · · *Fine* · · · D.C.

9.15 Allegro · · · France · · · *mf* · · · *Fine* · · · *f* · · · D.C.

D.C.

Section 3. The interval of the tritone.

9.23 Lento — Mexico

9.24 Moderato ma con moto — Poland

9.25 Allegro con spirito — Sweden

9.29

Allegro ma non troppo

Germany

9.30

Allegretto e marcato

Germany

Section 4. Other uses of diatonic intervals of the seventh.

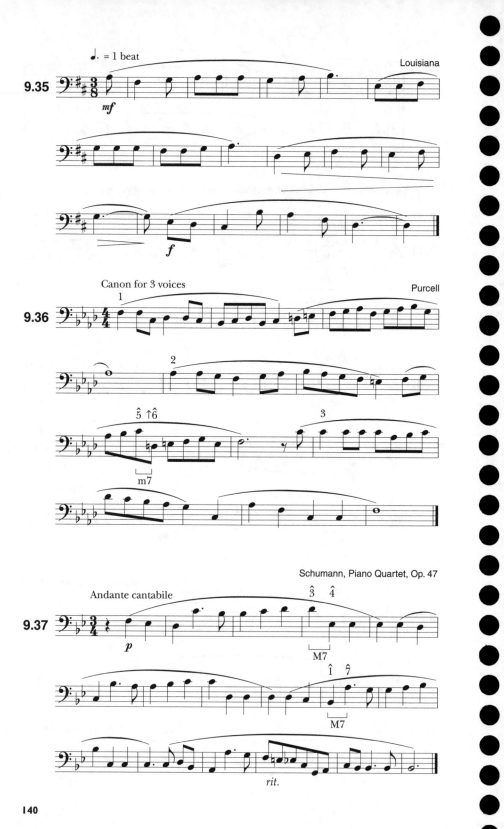

9.38

Section 5. Structured improvisation.

▶▶ Complete this melody using notes from the tonic triad and dominant seventh chord (as indicated below each bracket). Restrict yourself to rhythmic values no shorter than an eighth note.

9.39

▶▶ Complete this melody using elaborations of the tonic triad and dominant seventh chord (as indicated below each bracket). Use any combination of ♪, ♩, and ♩. that fits the meter.

9.40

▶▶ Complete this melody as indicated below each bracket. Include at least one leap of a minor seventh (between $\hat{5}$ and $\hat{4}$, either ascending or descending) both in measure 2 and in measure 5. Restrict yourself to rhythmic values no shorter than an eighth note and no longer than a half note.

include seventh leap

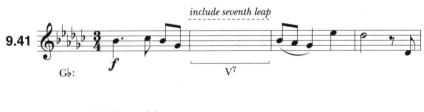

9.41

Gb:

include seventh leap

10

RHYTHM

the subdivision of the beat:
the simple beat into four parts,
the compound beat into six parts

RHYTHMIC READING, SIMPLE METERS

In simple meters, the beat may be subdivided into four parts—for example,

$$\frac{2}{4}\ \, \downarrow\ =\ \overline{} ,\ \ \frac{2}{2}\ \, \downarrow\ =\ \overline{} ,\ \ \frac{3}{8}\ \, \downarrow\ =\ \overline{} .$$

There are a variety of good rhythmic syllable systems that reflect the subdivided beat. Several popular systems are illustrated below; you may wish to use another approach.

a. Any note falling on the beat is given one syllable (such as *du*), any note falling halfway between beats (that is, on the "offbeat") is given another syllable (such as *de*), and any note that further subdivides the beat is given a different syllable (such as *ta*).

b. Each subdivision of the beat receives its own distinct syllable (such as *1-ee-and-ah*). The correct syllable is determined by a note's exact metrical position—that is, whether it falls on the first, second, third, or fourth subdivision.

c. Any note falling on the beat is named by the beat number, and all other notes are given the same neutral syllable (such as *ta*).

a.	du	de	du	de	du	ta	de	ta	du	de ta	du
b.	1	and	2	and	1	ee	and	ah	2	and ah	1
c.	1	ta	2	ta	1	ta	ta	ta	2	ta ta	1

Section 1. Preliminary exercises, simple meters.

Following are three groups of patterns, one each for the subdivisions of the ♩, 𝅗𝅥, and ♪ notes. Select first the group under the heading "♩ = 1 beat." Read each line in the group, repeating without interrupting the tempo until you have mastered it. Continue in like manner with the following line. When you have completed all the lines, skip from one line to any other line, as directed or as chosen, without interrupting the tempo. Continue with each of the other two groups in this same manner.

The patterns shown are those most commonly used. The rhythmic figures ♫. and ♫♩ (and comparable figures for other beat values) will be presented in Chapter 15, "Syncopation."

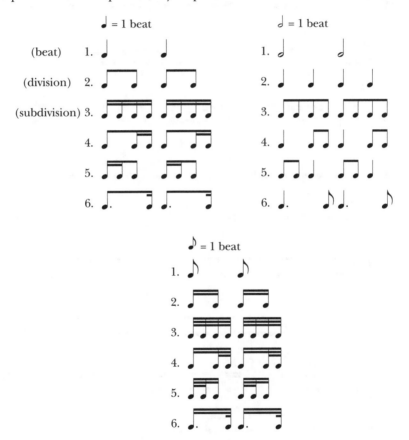

Section 2. Rhythmic reading exercises in simple meters.

143

10.3 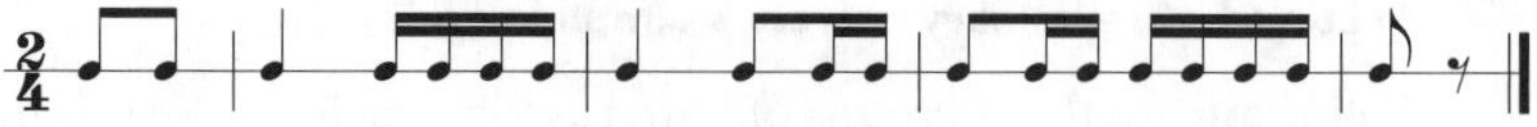

10.4 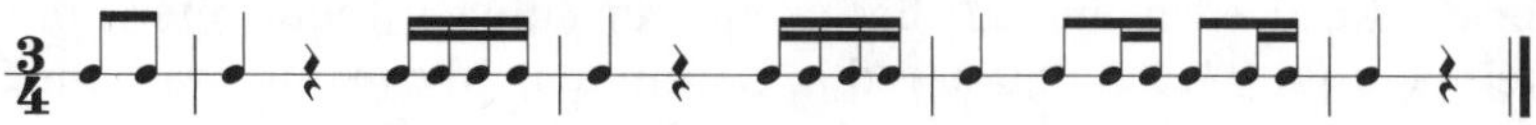

10.5 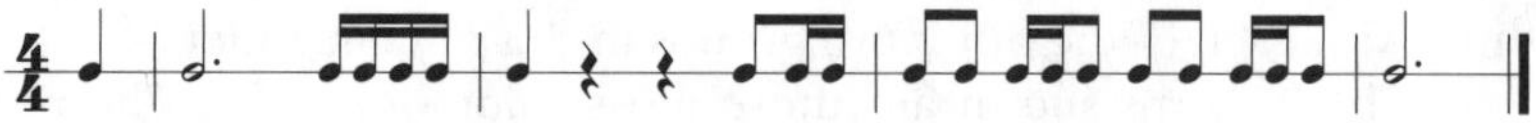

10.6 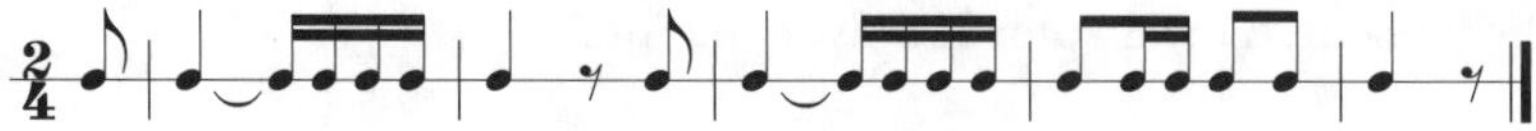

10.7 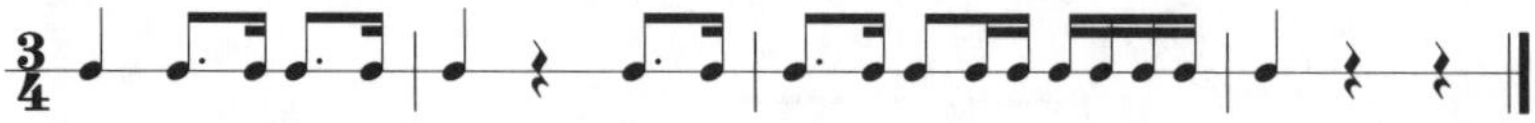

10.8 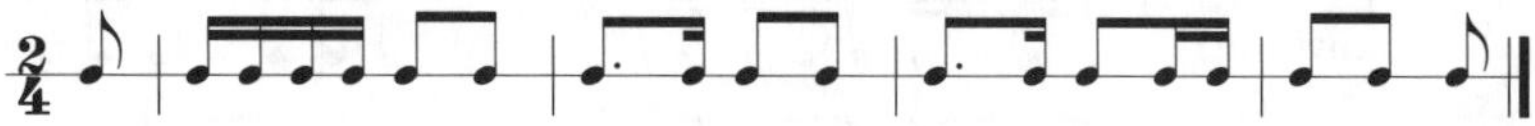

10.9 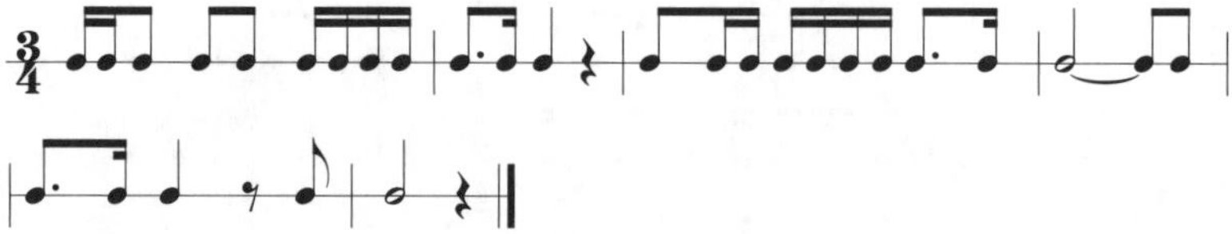

10.10 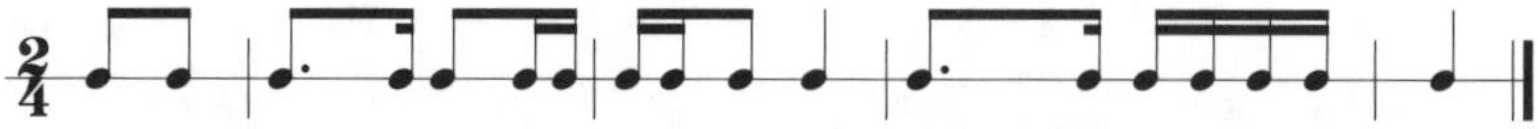

10.11 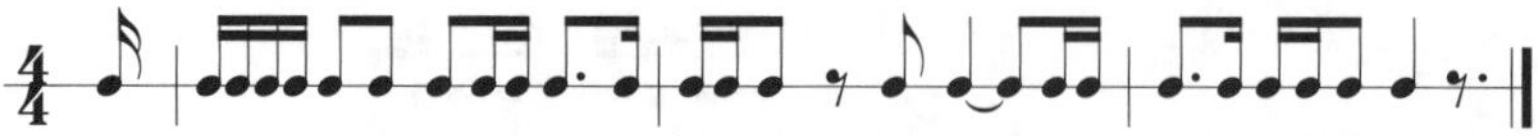

10.12 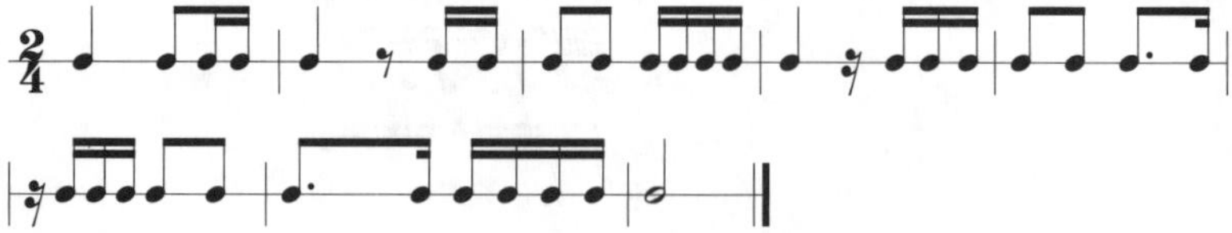

10.13 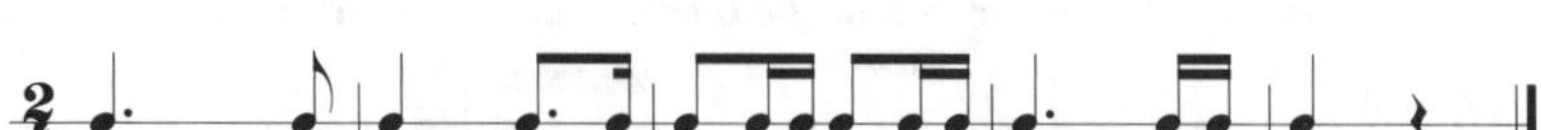

10.14 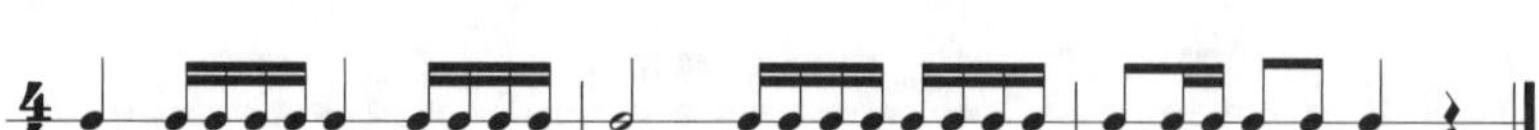

10.15
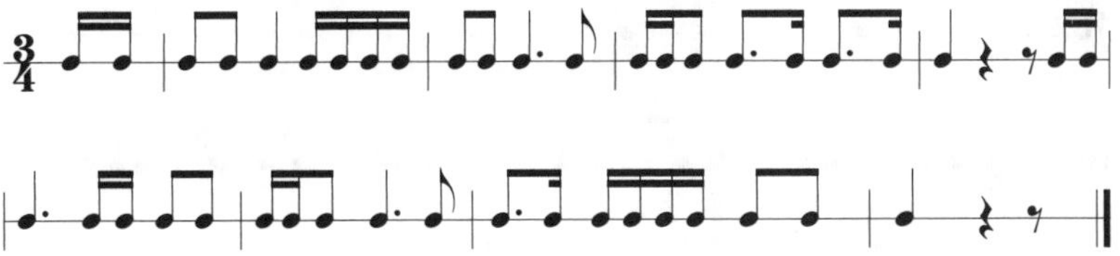

10.16
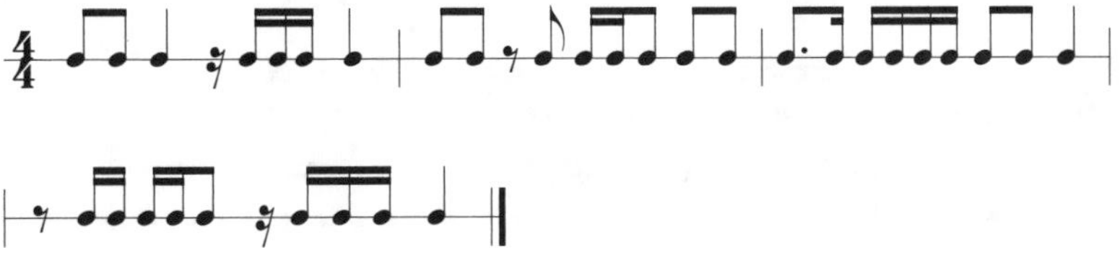

10.17
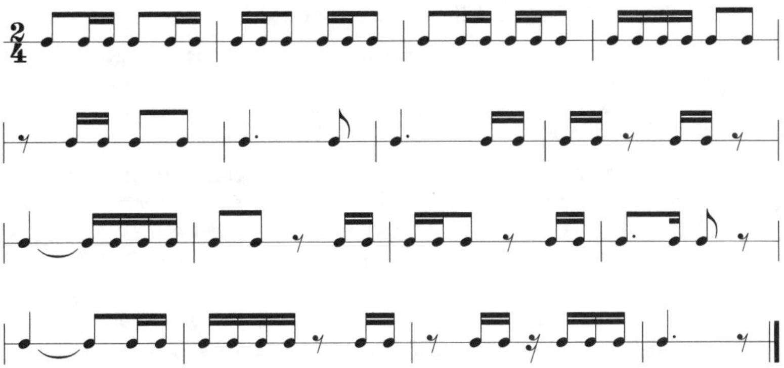

10.18
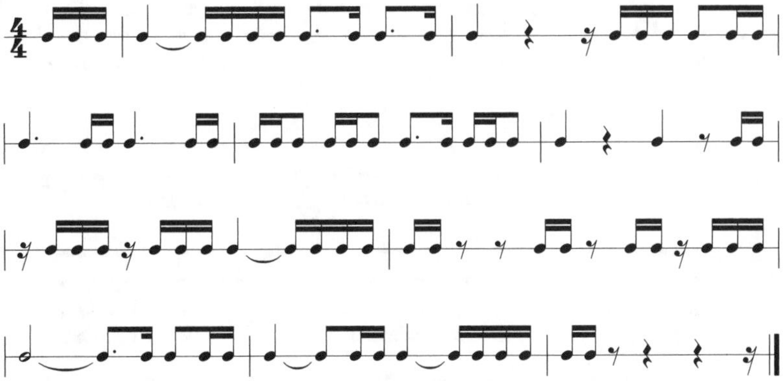

10.19
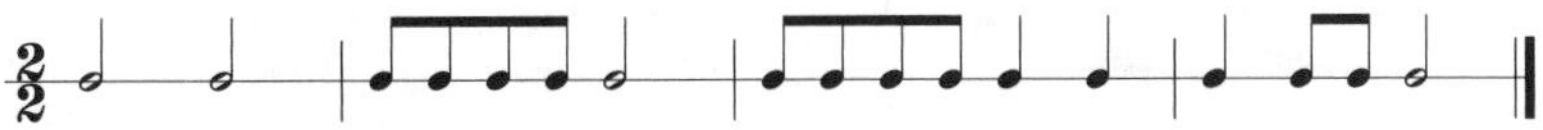

10.20
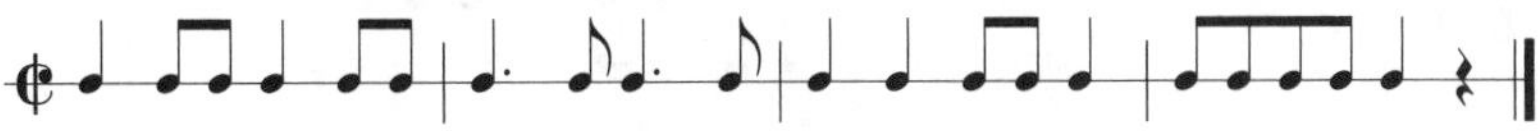

Section 3. Two-part drills, simple meters.

RHYTHMIC READING, COMPOUND METERS

In compound meters, the beat may be subdivided into six parts—for example,

$$\frac{6}{8} \; \texttt{♩.} = \texttt{♫♫♫}, \quad \frac{6}{4} \; \texttt{♩.} = \texttt{♫♫♫}, \quad \frac{6}{16} \; \texttt{♪} = \texttt{♫♫♫}.$$

Rhythmic syllable systems that reflect the metrical hierarchy are popular for performing subdivided rhythms in compound meters. This is probably because of the inherent challenges in using six distinct syllables. Several options (including one with different syllables for every subdivision) are shown below; you may wish to use another approach.

    a. Any note falling on the beat is given one syllable (such as *du*), the notes that divide the beat into thirds are given their own syllables (such as *da di*), and any note that further subdivides the beat is given a different syllable (such as *ta*).

    b. Any note falling on the beat is named by the beat number, the notes that divide the beat into thirds are given their own syllables (such as *la lee*), and any note that further subdivides the beat is given a different syllable (such as *ta*).

    c. Each subdivision of the beat receives its own distinct syllable (such as *ta va ki di da ma*). The correct syllable is determined by a note's exact metrical position—that is, whether it falls on the first, second, third, fourth, fifth, or sixth subdivision.

    d. Any note falling on the beat is named by the beat number, and all other notes are given the same neutral syllable (such as *ta*).

a.	du	da	di	du	ta	da	ta	di	ta	du_____	di ta du_____
b.	1	la	lee	2	ta	la	ta	lee	ta	1_____	lee ta 2_____
c.	ta	ki	da	ta	va	ki	di	da	ma	ta_____	da ma ta_____
d.	1	ta	ta	2	ta	ta	ta	ta	ta	1_____	ta ta 2_____

Section 4. Preliminary exercises, compound meters.

Follow directions for similar exercises in simple meters, page 143. The patterns in subdivision shown are the most common of those possible. Notice that beaming styles may vary.

Section 5. Rhythmic reading exercises in compound meters.

150

Section 6. Two-part drills, compound meters.

11

MELODY

intervals from the tonic and dominant triads

RHYTHM

subdivision in simple and compound meters

Section 1. Major keys.

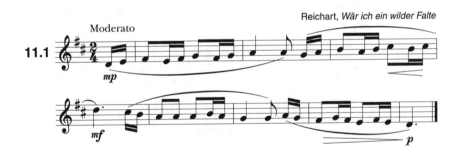

11.3   Con moto   England

11.4   Vif et gai   France

11.5   Allegro   Finland

11.6   Langsam   Schubert, *Wiegenlied*, D. 498

11.7 Allegretto   France

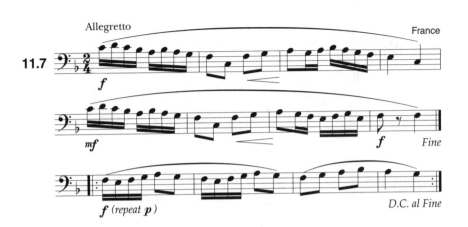

11.8 Tres vif   France

11.9 Canon for 5 voices   Praetorius

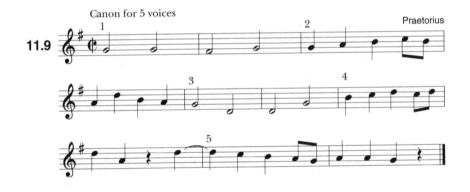

11.10 Dolendo   Nicaragua

11.11   (Stately)   Handel, *Teseo*

11.12   Andante   Ohio

11.13   Con moto   Texas

11.14   Allegro   Spain

11.15   Allegro   France

11.20 Canon for 4 voices — *1 2 3 4* — England

11.21 Lent — France — *mp*

11.22 Canon for 4 voices — *1 2 3 4* — Germany

Section 2. Minor keys.

11.23 Moderato — Mexico — *mp*

11.24 Allegro non troppo — Italy — *p*

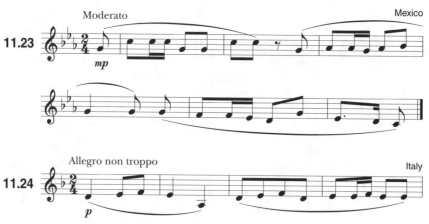

11.25 Andante — Scotland

11.26 Andante — England

11.27 Mesto — Ukraine

In melody 11.28, measure 3, the second note in the interval of the augmented second functions as an appoggiatura in the V^7 (F♯ A♯ C♯ E) harmony.

Section 3. Structured Improvisation.

➤➤ As indicated below each bracket, fill in the missing beats with an outline of the tonic triad, an outline of the dominant triad, or stepwise motion. A rhythm has been suggested in most places, but you will need to improvise your own rhythm in measure 7.

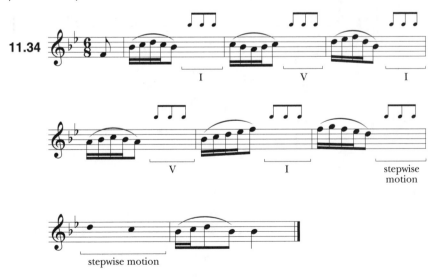

➤➤ A melodic outline for two phrases is provided below; notice that the two cadential measures have been completed. Using entirely stepwise motion and any combination of ♪ and ♩ that fits the meter, connect these notes (all of which fall on the beat) so that they form a complete melody. Look over the entire exercise and think about the key before you begin.

➤➤ Improvise a second phrase that "answers" the first (in other words, improvise a consequent phrase to the given antecedent phrase). It is appropriate for the second phrase to sound similar to the first phrase, perhaps even using an identical beginning. However, the final cadence must sound more conclusive.

12

MELODY

further use of diatonic intervals

RHYTHM

subdivision in simple and compound meters

Section 1. Diatonic intervals except the seventh and the tritone.

Mozart, String Quartet No.17, K. 458

12.7

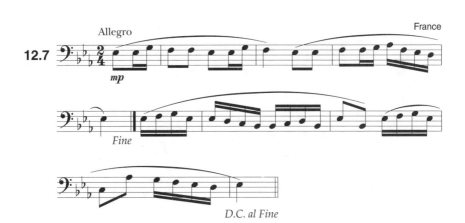

Allegro   France

mp

Fine

D.C. al Fine

12.8

Canon for 4 voices   Haydn

12.9

Canon for 2 voices   Germany

12.10

Moderato   Haydn, Symphony No. 100

p dolce

Canon for 3 voices

J. Hilton (17th century)

12.11

Allegro molto (♩ = 1 beat)

Cimarosa, *Il matrimonio segreto*

12.12

p

mf

Con moto

Germany (Brahms)

12.13

mf

p

mf

Fine

D.C. al Fine

Allegro

Mozart, *The Magic Flute*, K. 620

12.14

p

cresc. poco a poco

f

12.15 Con dolore   Scotland

p

mp

p

12.16 Moderato   Argentina

mp   cresc.

p   cresc.   mf

12.17 Andante   Wales

12.18 Allegretto   Grieg, *Lauf der Welt*

pp

rit.   *a tempo*

12.19 Teneramente   Stephen Foster, *The Village Maiden*

mp

mf

12.20   Allegretto   Grieg, *Holberg Suite*, Op. 40

12.21   Canon for 3 voices   Samuel Arnold (1740 –1802)

Haste thee_ nymph and bring with thee, jest and _ youth-ful_

jol - li - ty, Quips and _ cranks and wan - ton _ wiles,

nods and _ becks and wreath-ed smiles, Sport _ that _ wrink-led

care _ de - rides, and laugh - ter _ hold - ing both his sides.

12.22   Allegretto   Alabama

Couperin, *Soeur Monique*

Tendrement sans lenteur

12.27

Germany (Brahms)

Andante

12.28

Gounod, *Dites, la jeune belle*

Con moto

12.29

12.34 Alla marcia · · · · · · Germany

marcato

f

12.35 Giojoso · · Serbia

f

12.36 Allegro Telemann, *Tafel Musik*

p

mf

mf

12.37 Allegro appassionato Mendelssohn, Trio No. 2, Op. 66

mf sf

Largo sostenuto   Haydn, Quartet, Op. 33, No. 2

12.38

Bach, Motet, *Jesu, meine Freude*

12.39

Section 2. The dominant seventh (V⁷) chord; intervals of the seventh and the tritone.

12.40 Allegro — Handel, *Judas Maccabaeus*

12.41 Lively — France
Fine
D.C. al Fine

12.42 Allegretto — Germany

Canon for 3 voices   Salieri (1759–1825)

12.43

Con moto   Spain

12.44

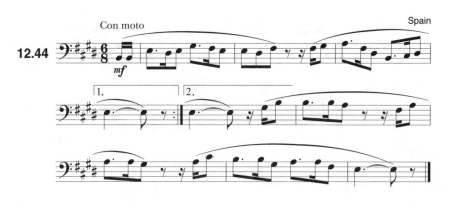

Energico   Poland

12.45

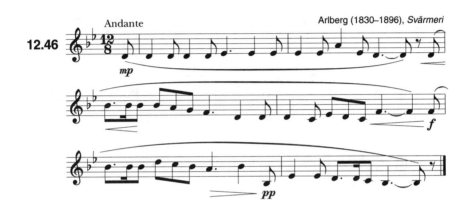

12.46 Andante   Arlberg (1830–1896), *Svärmeri*

12.47 Andante con moto   Mendelssohn, *Songs Without Words*, Op. 53

12.48 Poco allegretto   Lithuania

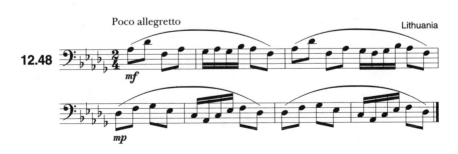

12.53 Canon for 3 voices — Couperin

12.54 Allegro — Martinique

Section 3. Other uses of the interval of the seventh.

Schnell   Germany

12.55

Allegretto   Poland

12.56

Sarabande   Bach, Klavier Suite in G Major (Orig.: G)

12.57

Bach, *Well-Tempered Clavier,* Vol. 1, Fugue 15

12.58

12.59 Mässig — Schubert, *Erntelied*

12.60 Largo — Poland

Section 4. Structured improvisation.

➤➤ A melodic outline is provided below. Using entirely stepwise motion and any combination of ♪ and ♩ that fits the meter, connect these notes (all of which fall on the beat) so that they form a complete melody.

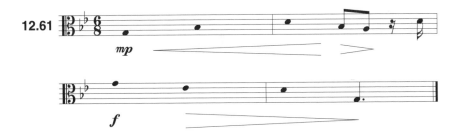

12.61

➤➤ Complete this melody, incorporating the opening neighbor-note motive as often as possible. Try to sustain a rhythm of steady sixteenth notes until the very end (where it is appropriate to use a longer note that falls on a beat).

12.62

d: i   V⁷

i   iv   V⁷   i

▶▶ Complete this melody, frequently including the opening motive (both the rhythm and the use of passing tones). Create an effective half cadence at the end of the first four-measure phrase and an authentic cadence at the end of the second four-measure phrase.

12.63

I   V⁷   (HC)

V⁷   I   ii   V⁷   I   (AC)

13

MELODY

Chromaticism (I)

chromatic nonharmonic tones;
the dominant
of the dominant (V/V) harmony;
modulation to the key of the dominant

Section 1. Chromatic nonharmonic tones. Augmented and diminished intervals created by their use.

Chromatic tones are those that are not members of the scale of the key in which the music sounds. Examples: In C major, F is diatonic, F♯ is chromatic; in D major, F♯ is diatonic, F𝄪 is chromatic; in E♭ major, A♭ is diatonic, A is chromatic. In its usual stepwise resolution, a raised chromatic tone moves up a half step to the next diatonic tone, and a lowered chromatic tone moves down a half step to the next diatonic tone.

The opening examples in this chapter show representative nonharmonic usages.

Passing tone, melody 13.1
Neighbor tone, melodies 13.2–13.3
Appoggiatura, melodies 13.4 (d4), and 13.5 (d3)
Double neighbors (or changing tones), melody 13.6

In the appoggiatura, the chromatic tone and the preceding tone will often produce an augmented or diminished interval such as the A2, d3, d4, A4, d5, and d7. Uses of ↑$\hat{6}$ and ↑$\hat{7}$ in a minor key may also create such intervals. To perform, sing the first note, then think the tone that follows the chromatic tone, and relate that chromatic tone to its following note. In melody 13.4, measure 3, you will see in F minor the tones A♭–E–F. Sing A♭, think F, and sing E–F.

Syllables for the chromatic scale include those for the seven diatonic notes and five additional syllables each for the ascending and descending forms of the scale.

13.4 Lento — France — *mp* — *mf* — Fine — D.C.

13.5 Allegretto — Joseph Steffan (1726–1797), *Gold'ne Freiheit* — *mf* — *f*

13.6 Moderato — Costa Rica — *mp* — *cresc.* — *mf* — *p*

13.7 Zärtlich — J. Ruprech, *An Röschen* (1785)

13.12

On what chromatically altered scale tone does this melody begin?

Mozart, Serenade, K. 239

13.13

Schubert, Mass in E♭

13.14

Section 2. The secondary dominant chord, V/V or V⁷/V. Modulation from a major key to its dominant key.

The presence of the raised tone #4̂ in a melody is often an indication of the use of secondary dominant harmony. In its frequent appearance at a cadence point, it implies either the half cadence V/V→V (C major: D F♯ A→G B D), or a modulation to the dominant (C major: F♯ is the leading tone in G major).

On paper, such a progression *looks* like a modulation, with the pivot chord I = IV, but it often *sounds* like a half cadence in the original key.

Choosing an analysis is not always easy, as the perception of reaching or not reaching a new key will differ from person to person. When hearing or performing such a progression, it helps to ask yourself, "Could the composition stop at this point or must it continue?" If the music must continue, considering the progression as a half cadence is most often the better choice.

The following melodies illustrate cadences on the dominant, each in turn more strongly emphasizing the dominant sound.

Melody 13.19: At the cadence (D–C#) of the second phrase, the implied harmonic progression, E G# B D→A C# E, *looks* like V^7→I in A major. But in listening, note that, in spite of the two occurrences of the E seventh chord, the *sound* suggests an immediate return to D major, particularly because the melody ends on the leading tone, C#, of the original key. Analysis as a secondary dominant progression is the better choice.

Melody 13.20: Here we have the same harmonic cadence as before. The root of the V chord, A, is now in the soprano. The "pull" back to D major is still considerable, though not as strong as in melody 13.19.

Melody 13.21: The implication of E G# B D→A C# E is heard twice in measures 5–8. Combined with the repetition, the final melody tone A can easily be heard as a new tonic tone, though hearing it as the dominant of D major cannot be dismissed.

Melody 13.22: Beginning in C major, the dominant harmony of G continues for eight measures after its first appearance and includes five V→I progressions in that key. Most listeners will probably hear a change of key, C major to G major.

Indisputable modulation to the dominant most frequently occurs in longer sections of compositions, such as movements from sonatas and symphonies, or in well-defined sections of smaller works.

The secondary dominant can also be found within the phrase in these contexts.

Melody 13.23: There is no chromatic sign in the melody to locate a new dominant sound. In measures 7–8, the logical harmonization is the half cadence B D♯ F♯ A→E G♯ B. When harmonized, the altered tone D♯ will be found in a lower voice.

Melody 13.24: In measure 14, the note B♮ locates the use of a single secondary dominant chord (V/V) within the phrase.

Moderato

Irving Berlin, "A Pretty Girl Is Like A Melody"

13.25

Trio (menuetto)

Mozart, Serenade, K. 100

13.26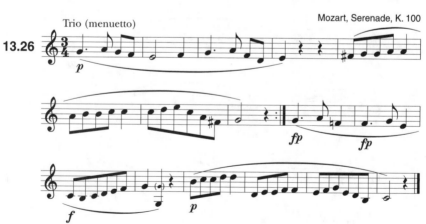

Anonymous, from *Noten-Büchlein vor Anna Magdalena Bach*

13.27

13.28 Ländler   Austria

13.29 Moderato   France

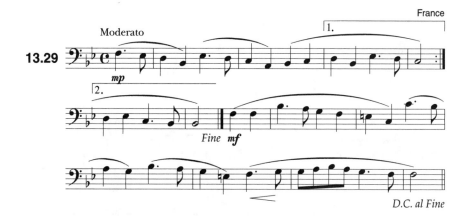

D.C. al Fine

13.30
Moderato

Germany (Brahms)

Fine

D.C. al Fine

13.31
Schnell

Germany

Fine

D.C. al Fine

13.32
Ziemlich lebhaft

Schubert, *Der Musensohn*

13.33
Langsam

Schubert, *Du bist die Ruh*

13.37 Ziemlich langsam   Schubert, *Tränenregen*

13.38 Ländler   Austria

13.39 Moderato Lully, *Armide*

13.40 Schubert, Minuet, D. 41, No. 18

13.41 Schubert, Minuet, D. 380, No. 1

Schubert, Minuet, D. 41

13.42

Beethoven, *Maigesang,* Op. 52, No. 4

13.43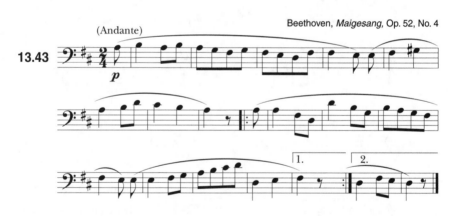

Scotland

13.44

13.45 Andante — Purcell, *The Fairy Queen*

13.46 Allegro — Mozart, *Sehnsucht nach dem Frühlinge,* K. 596

Canon for 4 voices

P. Hayes

13.47

Schumann, *Du Ring am meinem Finger,*
Op. 42, No. 4

13.48

Innig

p

D.C. al Fine

Larghetto   Mozart, Clarinet Quintet, K. 581

13.52

p

p

Nörmiger, *Tablaturbuch* (1598)

Largo

13.53

mp

Fine   *cresc.*

f   *D.C. al Fine*

13.60 Vivace — Telemann, *Die Ehre des Herrlichen*

f   *p*   *f*   *p*

cresc.

f

mp   *cresc.*   *f*

13.61 Allegretto — Mozart, *Zufriedenheit*

p

mp

Schumann, *Der Zeizig,* Op. 104, No. 4

13.62

Handel, *Jeptha*

13.63

13.69 Haydn, String Quartet, Op. 55, No. 2

13.70 Handel, *Xerxes*

Schumann, *Der Kartenlegerin*, Op. 31, No. 2

13.71

Beethoven, *Busslied*, Op. 48, No. 5

13.72

Section 3. Duets.

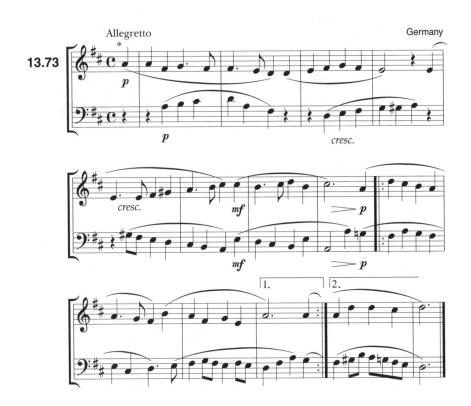

13.73

Allegretto   Germany

13.74

Moderato   Germany

Mozart, *Mass in C Minor*, K. 427

13.78

Mozart, *Così fan tutte*, K. 588

13.79

Allegretto

Mozart, String Quartet, K. 575

13.80

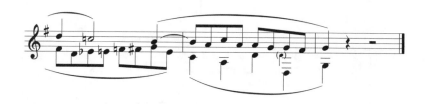

Allegro

Stamitz, Concerto für Basset Horn

13.81

Andante

Mozart, Symphony No. 38 *(Prague)*, K. 504

13.82

Section 4. Structured improvisation.

➤➤ A melodic outline for two phrases is provided below. Elaborate the given notes (all of which fall on the beat) with the opening measure's neighbor-note figure, using chromatic inflection whenever possible.

13.83

➤➤ A melodic outline for one phrase is provided below. Using entirely stepwise motion and any combination of ♪ and ♩ that fits the meter, connect these notes (all of which fall on the beat) so that they form a melody. Include some chromatic neighboring and/or passing tones.

13.84

▶▶ Complete the melody by outlining the harmonies indicated below each bracket. You may use notes outside the specified chords on metrically weak beats, provided that you approach and resolve them by step. A rhythmic pattern has been suggested in several locations.

14

MELODY

Chromaticism (II)

modulation to closely related keys; additional secondary dominant harmonies

In contrast to the nebulous quality of modulatory or secondary dominant progressions to the dominant, a modulation to any other key is usually more convincing, since its cadence usually has little or no inclination to return immediately to the original key. Of all the possible modulations to closely related keys,[1] those to the dominant, the relative major, and the relative minor are the most common. Note that from a minor key, the closely related dominant key is a *minor* key—for example, C minor to G *minor*.

Also in this chapter are examples of secondary dominant harmonies other than V/V—for example, in melody 14.1, measures 15–16, the progression V/ii→ii (A major: F♯ A♯ C♯ →B D F♯).

---

[1] When the signatures of two keys are the same, or differ by not more than one sharp or one flat, the keys are considered *closely* related. Examples:

from C major to D minor (1♭)	from C minor to E♭ major (3♭)
to E minor (1♯)	to F minor (4♭)
to F major (1♭)	to G minor (2♭)
to G major (1♯)	to A♭ major (4♭)
to A minor (0♯ or ♭)	to B♭ major (2♭)

Section I. Single-line melodies.

14.1 Allegro   Schubert, *An den Frühling*

V/ii   cresc.   ii   *p*   cad.⁶₄   V

I

14.2 Adagio   Germany

V

i

mf   *p*

14.3 Adagio   Germany (Brahms)

p   *mp*

14.4 Allegro   Germany

14.5 Langsam   Schubert, *Das Zügenlächlein*

14.6 Allegro   Handel, *Deidamia*

14.7 Langsam — Germany (Brahms)

14.8 Andantino — Brazil

14.9 Allegro 𝄋 — Purcell, *King Arthur*

Fine

D.S. al Fine

14.10 Andante — Liszt, *Angiolin dal biondo crin*

pp dolce

poco rit. *a tempo*

poco rit.

14.11 Canon for 3 voices — Beethoven

14.12 Moderato — Netherlands

mp

f

mp

223

14.13 Allegro molto — Beethoven, String Quartet, Op. 18, No. 2

14.14 Andantino — Germany

14.15 Allegro moderato — Purcell, *Dido and Aeneas*

cresc.

f

D.S. al Fine

Andante

Gounod, *Faust*

14.16

p

Gut zu declamiren

Schumann, *Myrten,* "Rätsel," Op. 25, No. 16

14.17

mf

Giocoso

Virgin Islands

14.18

mp

mf

1.

2.

Andante

Durante (1684–1755), *Vergin Tutto Amor*

14.19

14.20 Allegro   Fauré, *Fleur Jetée*

14.21 Andante   Beethoven, *Sehnsucht*, Op. 83, No. 2

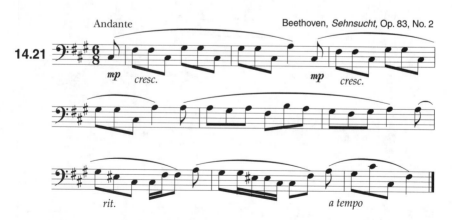

14.25 Lento   France

14.26 Presto   Haydn, String Quartet, Op. 76, No. 5

14.27 Allegro moderato   Mozart, Sonata for Violin, K. 40

Brahms, *Zigeunerlieder,* Op. 105, No. 3

14.28

Allegro giocoso

Andante

Reichardt, *Der Strauss*

14.29

Lully, *Le marriage forcé*

Gavotte

14.30

Canon for 3 voices

Cranford (17th century)

14.31

Schumann, String Quartet, Op. 41, No. 3

14.32

Allegro

Andante

Mozart, *La Clemenza di Tito*, K. 621

14.33

14.34

Mit innigkeit

Germany

14.35

Andantino

Franz, *Mutter, o sing mich zur Ruh!*

14.36

Canon for 3 voices

Couperin

14.37 Andante con moto — Haydn, String Quartet, Op. 71, No. 3

14.38 Andante espressivo — France

14.39 Andante con moto — Schubert, *Rosamunde*, Op. 26

Mendelssohn, *Romanze,* Op. 8, No. 11

14.40

Schumann, *Schlusslied des Narren,*
Op. 127, No. 5

14.41

14.47 Allegro   Handel, *Teseo*

D.C.

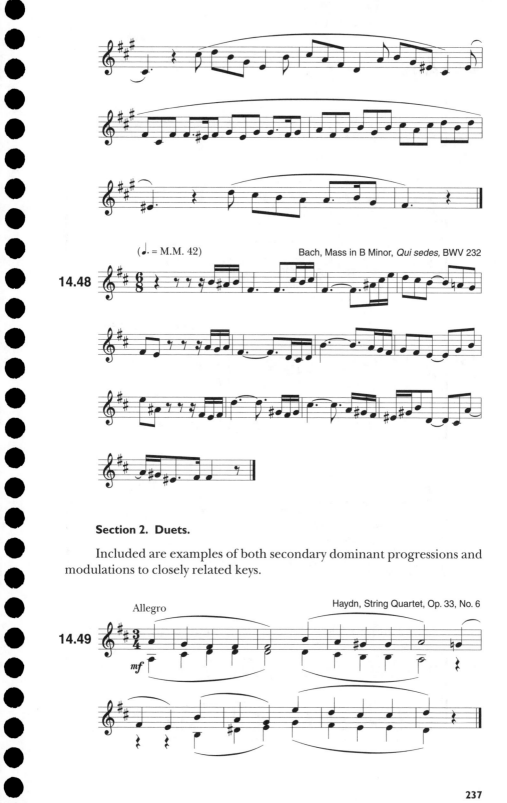

(♩. = M.M. 42)   Bach, Mass in B Minor, *Qui sedes,* BWV 232

14.48

Section 2. Duets.

Included are examples of both secondary dominant progressions and modulations to closely related keys.

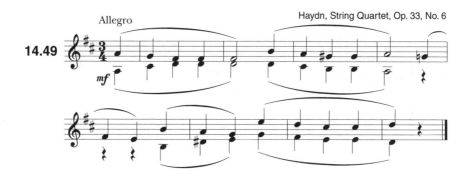

Allegro   Haydn, String Quartet, Op. 33, No. 6

14.49

14.50 Haydn, *The Creation*
Allegro

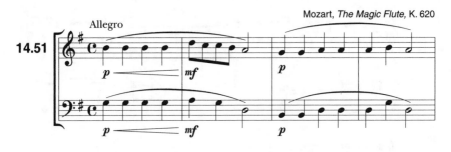

14.51 Mozart, *The Magic Flute*, K. 620
Allegro

14.52 Haydn, String Quartet, Op. 76, No. 1
Allegro con spirito

14.53

Moderato

Haydn, *Theresienmesse*

Do - mi - ne, Do - mi - ne De - us,

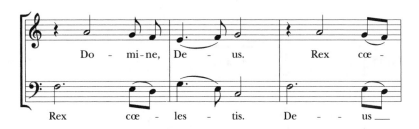

Do - mi - ne, De - us. Rex cœ -

Rex cœ - les - tis. De - us ___

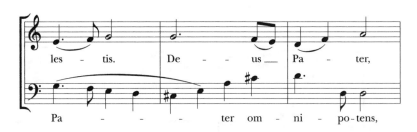

les - tis. De - us ___ Pa - ter,

Pa - ter om - ni - po - tens,

De - us Pa - ter om - ni - po - tens.

De - us Pa - ter om - ni - po - tens.

14.54 Tenderly Schumann, *Schön Blümelein,* Op. 43, No. 3

14.55 H. Albert, *Cras serum est vivere* (1638)

14.59

Largo e piano

Handel, *Julius Caesar*

14.60

Vivace

Dittersdorf, *Doktor und Apotheker*

14.61

Adagio   Corelli, Sonata da Chiesa, Op. 3, No. 2

Andante moderato   Mozart, Mass in C Minor, K. 427

14.62

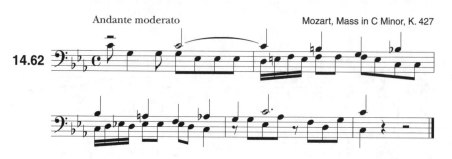

Larghetto   Handel, *Ariodante*

14.63

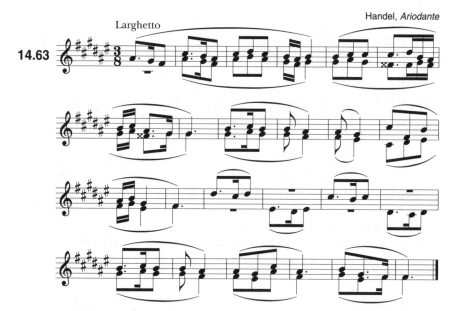

Presto   Bach, *Brandenburg Concerto No. 4*

14.64

14.65 Moderato — Rubenstein, *Volkslied*

14.66 Im Ländler tempo — Brahms, *Liebeslieder Walzer,* Op. 52

Vivaldi, Trio Sonata, Op. 1, No. 2

14.67

M. Cazzati, Trio Sonata (1656)

14.68

Section 3. Structured improvisation.

➤➤ Complete the partial melody below as indicated. Notice that measure 2 will modulate to the relative major, then measure 3 will gradually return to the original minor key. (Helpful hint: an A♯ in measure 3 will make the return to the relative minor more convincing.)

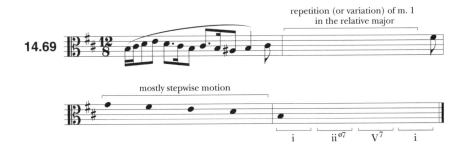

➤➤ Complete the given melody, following the harmonies indicated below the brackets. You may simply arpeggiate the chords, or you may elaborate them with passing tones and neighboring tones. Restrict yourself to rhythmic values no shorter than an eighth note.

➤➤ Improvise two phrases according to the outline below. The notes provided should fall on the beat, and your melody should elaborate the harmonies shown below the brackets. Notice that the second phrase modulates to the key of the dominant; the perfect authentic cadence indicated at the end is in the new key.

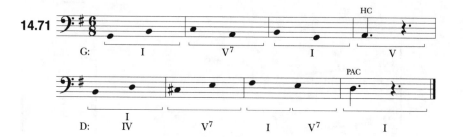

15

RHYTHM AND MELODY

syncopation

Syncopation occurs when the normal metrical pattern of accentuation is deliberately contradicted. Syncopation can be created by

1. Accenting a weak beat or a weak part of a beat:

2. Tying a weak beat into the next strong beat:[1]

3. Tying the weak division of a beat into the next beat:

---

[1] Some passages seemingly in syncopation may be subject to a different interpretation. For example, the pattern ♩♪♪♪♪♪|♪ ♪♪♪♪♪| is often performed as ♩♩ ♩ ♩♩♩|♩ ♩ ♩♩|, a device known as *hemiola*. See Chapter 17, page 316.

RHYTHMIC READING

Section I. Divided beat patterns in simple meters.

Section 2. Divided beat patterns in compound meters.

251

Section 3. Two-part drills.

253

Section 4. Subdivided beat patterns in simple meters.

Section 5. Subdivided beat patterns in compound meters.

Section 6. Two-part drills.

SIGHT SINGING

Section 7. Divided beat patterns in simple meters.

Melodies 15.70–15.81: Diatonic; no note value shorter than the divided beat.

Melodies 15.82–15.84: Diatonic; subdivision of the beat included, but not in patterns of syncopation.

Melodies 15.85–15.95: Chromatic tones and subdivision included.

15.77 Allegro — Piccini, *Allesandro nelle Indie*

15.78 Allegretto — Dominican Republic

15.79 Allegro assai — Haydn, Divertimento

15.80 Andante — Spiritual, United States

15.81

Allegro ♩. = 36   Beethoven, String Quartet, Op. 18, No. 6

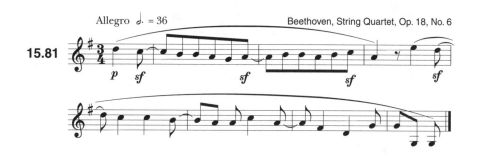

15.82

Muffat (1690–1770), Suite for Harpsichord

Allegro

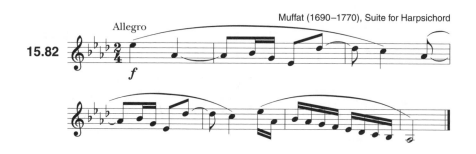

15.83

Poco allegretto   Romania

Canon for 3 voices

Caldara

15.84

Sarabande

Purcell, Suite V

15.85

Canon for 3 voices

Caldara

15.86

15.87 Adagio — Haydn, Symphony in F♯ Minor (1772)

15.88 Allegro — Vivaldi, Concerto for Two Violins

15.89 Presto — Mozart, Symphony No. 38 *(Prague)*, K. 504

15.90

Beethoven, String Quartet, Op. 18, No. 5

Trio

15.91

Beethoven, String Quartet, Op. 59, No. 2

Allegretto

15.92

Brazil

Allegro

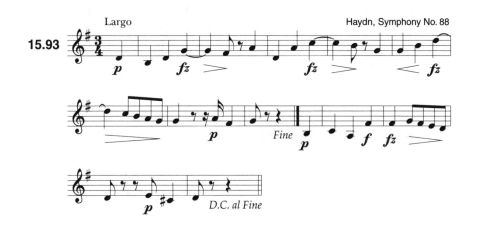

15.93 Largo — Haydn, Symphony No. 88

15.94 Marcia — Berlin, "I've Got My Captain Working for Me Now"

Schubert, *German Dance*, D. 973, No. 3

15.95

Section 8. Divided beat patterns in compound meters.

In the rhythmic figure ♪♩, the strong beat (first note) is usually accented, as in melody 15.96, measure 1 (similar to ♫., the so-called *Scotch snap* in simple meters). If the second note of the figure is to be accented, it is marked with a sign such as > or *sf*, as in melody 15.97.

15.96

15.97

15.102 Fast ($\flat$. = 1 beat)   Arizona

15.103 Assai agitato $\flat$. = 180   ($\flat$. = 1 beat)   Schumann, String Quartet, Op. 41, No. 3

15.104

Giga (♩. = 1 beat)

Pasquini, *Canzone Francese*

15.105

Allegro molto (♩ = 1 beat)

Beethoven, Cello Sonata, Op. 69, No. 3

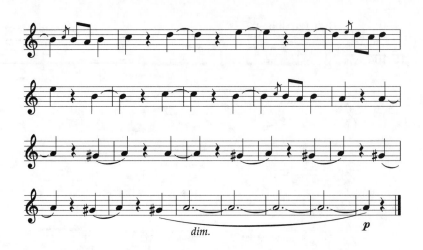

dim.   **p**

Section 9. Duets.

15.106   Allegretto   Bohemia

mf

Fine

f

D.C. al Fine

15.107   Presto   Haydn, Symphony No. 52

p

15.108

Con spirito

Jamaica

15.109

Andantino

Mozart, *Luisita amabile,* K. 480

15.110   Dvořák, String Quartet, Op. 51

Vivace ♩. = 86

15.111   Haydn, String Quartet, Op. 74, No. 1

Vivace

15.112   Allegro   Haydn, String Quartet, Op. 20, No. 6

sempre sotto voce

15.113   Handel, Trio Sonata, Op. 5, No. 4

15.114   Allegro   Mozart, Symphony No. 10, K. 74

(f)

15.115

(Allegro)   Handel, Sonata for Flute and Continuo

* Continuo may be sung and/or realized at the keyboard.

Section 10. Subdivided beat patterns in simple and compound meters.

15.116 Not fast — Scott Joplin, *The Easy Winners*

15.117 Allegro moderato — Brazil — *mf*

15.118 Allegro — Alabama

15.119 Moderato — Florida

15.120 Allegro — South Carolina

15.121 Allegretto — England

277

15.126 Spiritual, United States

15.127 Spiritual, United States

15.128 Spiritual, United States

15.129 Moderato — Dominican Republic

15.130 Andante grazioso — Scotland

15.131 Con moto — Trinidad

Section 11. Structured improvisation.

➤➤ Maintaining the syncopated rhythm established in the opening measures, complete this melody by outlining the chords indicated below the brackets.

15.135

➤➤ Complete the melody below using syncopated rhythms like the one provided in measure 1. You may simply outline the triads indicated, or you may elaborate them with passing and neighboring tones.

15.136

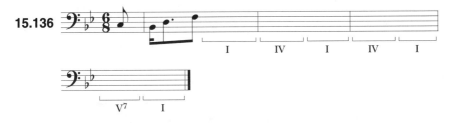

➤➤ Improvise a consequent phrase that "answers" the given antecedent phrase. It is appropriate for the second phrase to sound similar to the first phrase, perhaps even using an identical beginning. However, the final cadence must sound more conclusive.

15.137

16

RHYTHM AND MELODY

triplet division of undotted note values; duplet division of dotted note values

A triplet division of an undotted note value is indicated by three notes with a "3" added. The division of three uses the same note value as that for the usual division into two parts (for example, $\quarternote = \eighthnote\eighthnote = \overset{3}{\eighthnote\eighthnote\eighthnote}$).

Triplet Division

Undotted Note Value	Division into 2	Division into 3	Division into 6

The duplet division of a dotted note can be indicated in three ways:

1. Most commonly, two notes with a "2," using the same note value as the division of three ($\dottedquarternote = \eighthnote\eighthnote\eighthnote = \overset{2}{\eighthnote\eighthnote}$).

2. Less commonly, two notes with a "2," using the same note value as the one being divided ($\overset{2}{\sqcap}$). See melody 16.70, shown as (=).

3. Found mostly in twentieth-century music, two dotted notes of the next smaller value ($\sideset{}{}{}$ and $\sideset{}{}{}$). An example of can be seen in melody 21.57, among others, in Chapter 21.

Duplet Division

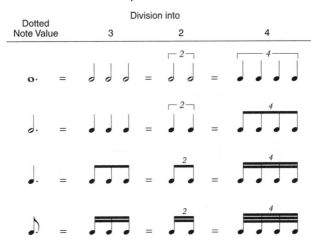

RHYTHMIC READING

Section I. Triplet division of undotted note values.

In example 16.1, *a* and *b* sound identical when performed at the same tempo. The triplet in simple meter could be said to be "borrowed" from compound meter, since it sounds exactly the same as the normal division of three in compound meter.

16.4

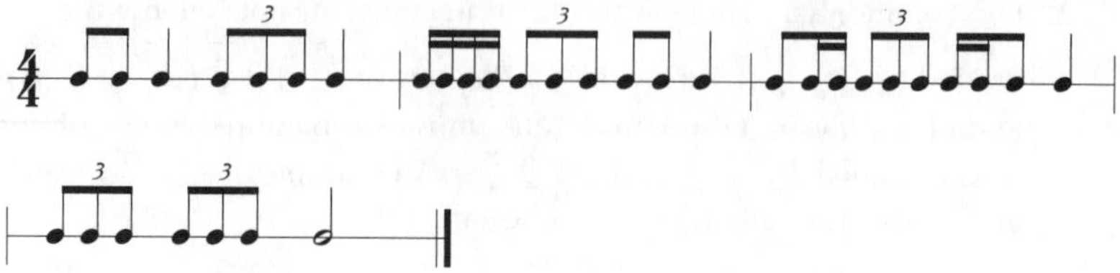

16.5

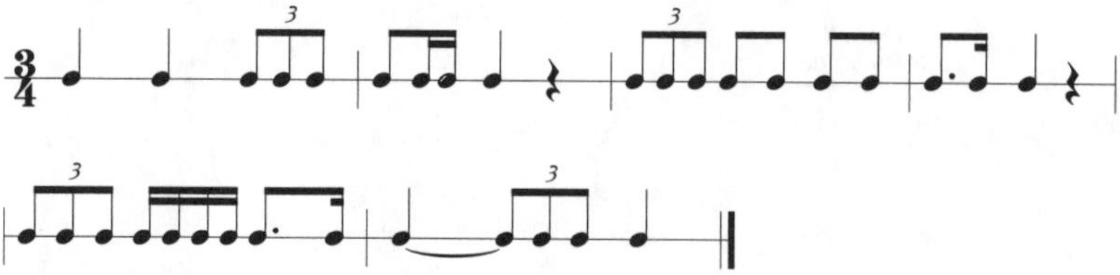

16.6

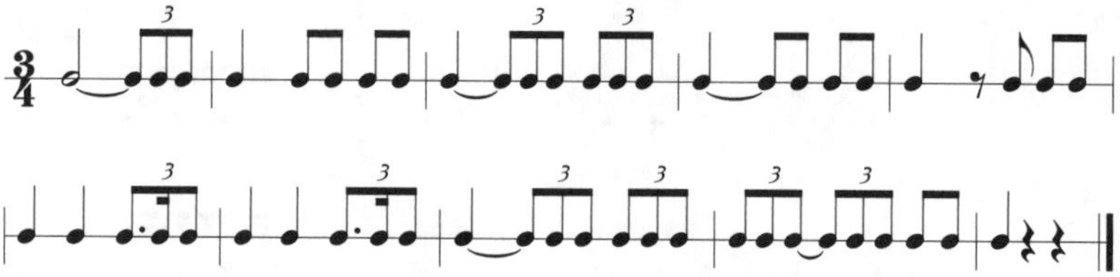

16.7

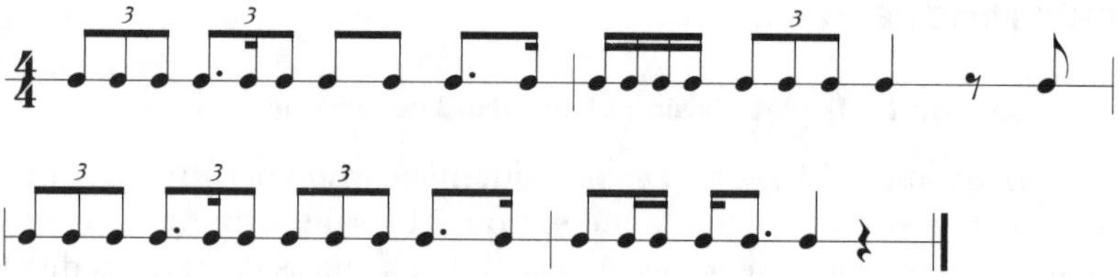

16.8

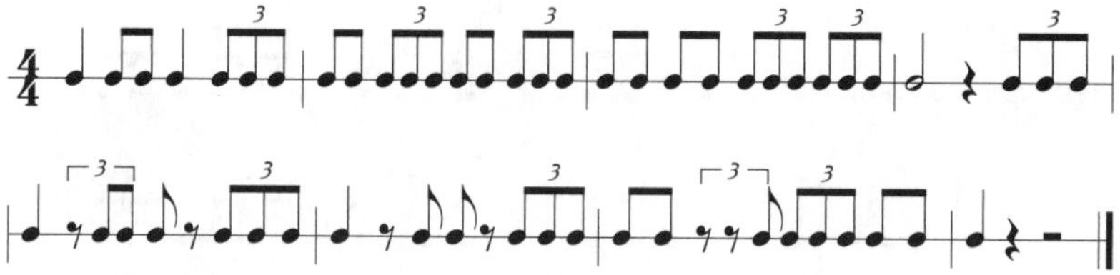

16.9

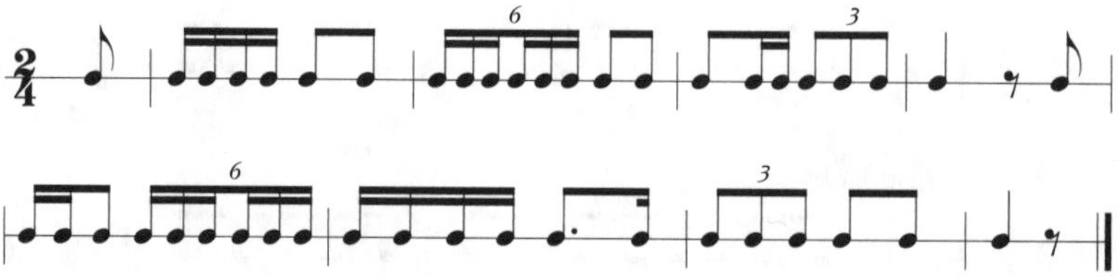

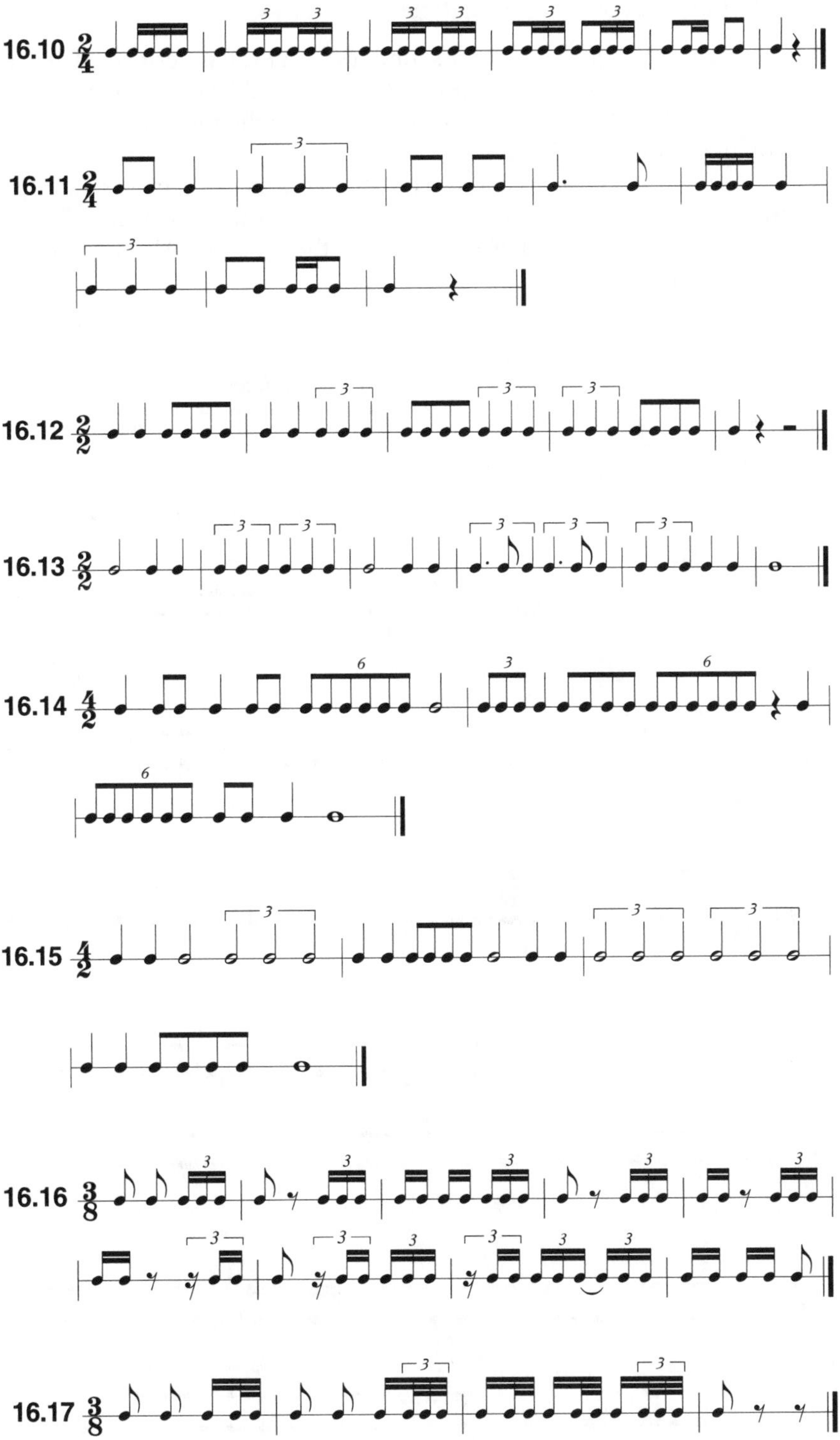
16.10
16.11
16.12
16.13
16.14
16.15
16.16
16.17

Section 2. Duplet division of dotted note values.

In example 16.18, *a, b,* and *c* sound identical when performed at the same tempo. The duplet in compound meter could be said to be "borrowed" from simple meter, since it sounds exactly the same as the normal division of two in simple meter.

At *c*, the duplet notation as two dotted eighth notes is mathematically accurate. Each dotted eighth note is equivalent to three sixteenth notes, exactly one-half of the six sixteenth notes in the measure. This notation is less commonly used.

Section 3. Two-part drills.

The goal of these drills is the ability to perform simple and compound rhythmic units simultaneously, a common situation for keyboard players, as well as for any musician performing a part in one meter while another meter is sounding.

In examples 16.29 and 16.30 (simple meter signature), think simple and then compound as you alternate hands. Repeat until the transition from one to the other is easily accomplished, then go past the repeat bar, performing simple and compound units simultaneously.

In examples 16.31 and 16.32 (compound meter signature), follow the same procedure, alternating your thinking and performing, first in compound meter and then in simple meter, followed by simultaneous performance of the two meters.

16.33

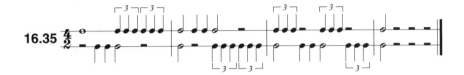

16.34

16.35

16.36

SIGHT SINGING

Section 4. Triplet division of undotted note values.

Dvořák, String Quartet, Op. 106

16.37

16.38

Con spirito

Arizona

Con moto

Mendelssohn, *O for the Wings of a Dove*

16.39

Schumann, *Frühlingsbotschaft,* Op. 79, No. 3

16.40

Wagner, *Rienzi*

16.41

Schubert, *Wasserflut,* Op. 89, No. 6

16.42

(stark)

16.43 Presto ma non troppo — Chopin, Mazurka, Op. 7, No. 4

16.44 Allegro deciso — Berlioz, *Benvenuto Cellini*

cresc.

sf

16.45 Moderato — Schubert, *Am Strome*, Op. 8, No. 4

mp

pp

16.52 Beethoven, Piano Sonata, Op. 7

Poco allegretto

16.53 Verdi, *Rigoletto*

Allegro agitato

Meno mosso

16.58 Spiritual, United States

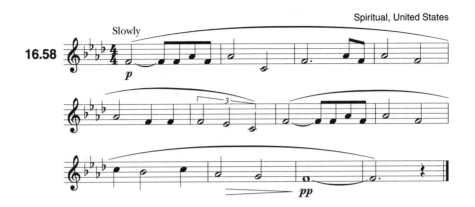

16.59 Slovakia

16.60 Venezuela

Section 5. Duplet division of dotted note values.

16.61 Moderato — Utah

16.62 Allegro — Grieg, *Das Dichters Gesang*

16.63 Assez animé — France

16.64 Moderato — Pennsylvania

16.65 ♪. = 108 — Texas

16.66 Lebhaft — Brahms, *Guter Rat*, Op. 75

16.71 Allegro — Franz, *Genesung*

16.72 Allegro apassionato — Grieg, *To Spring*

16.73   Allegro   Spain

Schumann, *Der schwere Abend*, Op. 90, No. 6

16.74

Section 6. Duets.

16.75   Andante   Germany

16.76 Con spirito · Germany

16.77 Con moto · Germany

Andante

Binchois (c.1400–1460), *Missa Angelorum*

16.80

Et in spir - i - tum _____ sanc - tum Do - mi -
Et in spir - i - tum _____ sanc - tum Do - mi -

num _____ et vi - vi - fi - -
num _____ et vi -

can - - tem qui ex pa - tre
vi - fi - can - tem _____ qui ex pa -

fi - li - o - que pro - ce - dit.
tre fi - li - o - que pro - ce - - dit.

Allegretto

Schumann, *Faust,* Op. 148

16.81

sempre *p*

sempre *p*

Brahms, String Quintet, Op. 88

16.82

Brahms, *Spätherbst,* Op. 92

16.83

Section 7. Structured improvisation.

➤➤ Elaborate the harmony indicated below each bracket using passing tones and chordal skips similar to the first measure (but not necessarily maintaining the same contour in each measure). Include at least one triplet per measure.

➤➤ By maintaining coherent melodies in different registers, exercise 16.85 implies two distinct voices. The effect is essentially like a duet, but with only one performer. Complete the melody by elaborating the two-voice outline provided, similar to the way in which the first measure elaborates B♭–G (shown above the staff). Leap between the two implied voices at least once in each measure, and try to include several triplets.

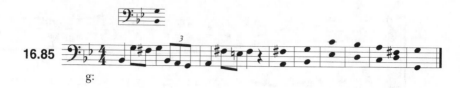

16.85

g:

▶▶ The melody initiated below will create a sequence, assuming it is continued as indicated. A sequence is the repetition of a pattern (melodic or harmonic—often both) at different pitch levels; for an example, see melody 9.38. Notice that as you repeat the established pattern beginning on different scale degrees, the interval qualities may change to fit the key—for instance, a whole step may become a half step, or a minor third may become a major third. (Helpful hint: it is appropriate to raise $\hat{7}$ when returning to the tonic, but generally not otherwise. Thus, you will want to include ↑$\hat{7}$ in measure 7, but not in the middle of the sequence. Keep the melodic minor scale in mind near the end in order to avoid an augmented second.)

16.86

f♯:

Now create your own sequence based on the same harmonic framework. Create an initial pattern that outlines the first two chords, then move the pattern down by step until you reach the tonic again at the end. It is perfectly acceptable to elaborate your basic pattern and/or alter its last repetition in order to create a stronger cadential effect.

Basic harmonic framework for this sequence:

Major key	I	IV	vii°	iii	vi	ii	V	I
Minor key	i	iv	VII	III	VI	ii°	V	I

Diatonic chords are often replaced by a secondary dominant chord with the same root. For instance, as the exercise above illustrates, V⁷/iv might substitute for i.

17

RHYTHM AND MELODY

changing meter signatures; the hemiola; less common meter signatures

RHYTHMIC READING

Section I. Definitions and rhythmic reading exercises.

Changing meters (melodies 17.28–17.39). One or more changes of meter may occur within a composition. Most commonly, the changes occur all within simple meter or all within compound meter, the denominators of the signatures remaining constant. Consequently, the duration of the beat is the same in each meter. A new meter signature is placed at the point of each change.

When the change is from simple meter to compound meter, or the reverse, there are two distinct possibilities:

1. The divisions of the two meters are of equal duration (often indicated in the score by a symbol such as ♪ = ♪ at the point of the change). Example 17.3 shows that the eighth note of ⅜ is equal in value to the eighth note of ¾. For this particular type of change, however, such symbols may be omitted.

2. When a symbol such as ♩ = ♩. appears, the durations of the two note values are equal. In example 17.7a, the quarter note of ¾ is equal in duration to the dotted quarter note of ⅜. Example 17.7b shows how the same rhythmic sound can be notated with the use of triplets.

310

A double signature combines the two signatures to be used during the composition. After the double signature $\frac{3}{8}\frac{2}{4}$, for example, each measure will be either $\frac{3}{8}$ or $\frac{2}{4}$ without further indication. Such a signature often indicates a regular alternation between the two meters—$\frac{3}{8}\frac{2}{4}\frac{3}{8}\frac{2}{4}$—or a pattern of successive meters, such as $\frac{3}{8}\frac{3}{8}\frac{2}{4}\frac{3}{8}\frac{2}{4}\frac{2}{4}$. Triple signatures such as $\frac{4}{4}\frac{2}{4}\frac{3}{4}$ are possible but rare.

The *hemiola* (melodies 17.40–17.51) is a change of grouping that suggests a change of meter without the use of a changing meter signature. In this device, two successive groups of three beats (or three divisions) create the aural impression of three groups of two beats (or two divisions)—for instance, ♩♩♩ ♩♩♩ becomes ♩♩ ♩♩ ♩♩.

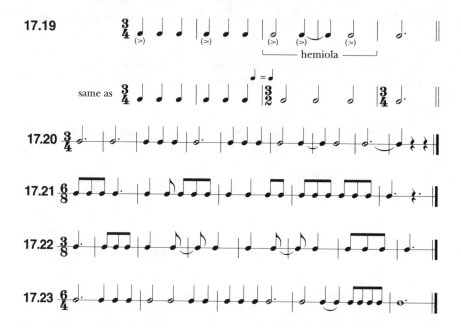

Meters of 5 and 7 (melodies 17.52–17.73). These time signatures usually sound like two alternating meters, such as $\frac{5}{4} = \frac{3}{4}\frac{2}{4}$ or $\frac{2}{4}\frac{3}{4}$, or $\frac{7}{8} = \frac{4}{8}\frac{3}{8}$ or $\frac{3}{8}\frac{4}{8}$. The beat groupings are usually reflected by the notation, such as ♩♩♩ ♩♩ for 3 + 2. The 3 + 4 grouping of melody 17.66 is indicated by a dotted bar line within each measure. A constant alternation can be indicated by a signature such as $\frac{3+2}{4}$.

Other meter signatures are uncommon in music before the twentieth century; they must be interpreted on an individual basis.

SIGHT SINGING

Section 2. Changing meter signatures.

17.32 Andante grazioso — Brahms, Piano Trio, Op. 101

p dolce

1.   2.

17.33 Con brio — Portugal

f

mp

f

p

pp

17.34 Allegro — France

mf

Canon for 3 voices

J. Nares (18th century)

17.39

1

Wilt thou lend me thy mare to go a mile? —

No! she's lame leap-ing o - ver a style.

2

But if thou wilt her to me _____ spare,

Thou shalt have mon - ey for _____ thy mare.

3

Oh! ho! _____ say you so?

Mon-ey will make my mare to go; Mon-ey will make my mare to go!

Section 3. The hemiola.

Example 17.40 demonstrates the "classic" sound and notation for the hemiola: one or more three-beat groupings followed by a group of three two-beat groupings. Their notation and placement in context vary widely, as can be seen in these melodies, but each expresses a 3–2 or 2–3 relationship.

17.41. In ⅜: two groups of three eighth notes are followed by a group of three quarter notes within one measure of ¾.

17.42. The 3–2 relationship reversed: three groups of two eighth notes are followed by two groups of three eighth notes (2–3).

17.43. There are two successive groups of hemiolas.

17.44. The cadence usually expected for ¾, measures 7–8, is preceded by three successive groups of two. The accompanying score for one piano, four hands, is in strictly triple simple time, in contrast to the hemiolas.

The hemiola was used frequently in the seventeenth and eighteenth centuries but saw declining interest in the nineteenth century, except in the music of Johannes Brahms and Hugo Wolf. The twentieth century saw its increased usage along with similar devices that expressed the revival of rhythmic freedom.

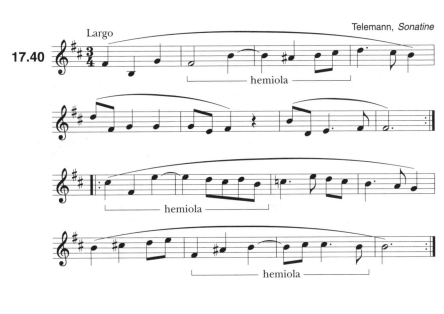

17.45 Allegro molto   Mexico

17.46 Allegro   Bach, Sonata for Flute and Clavier No. 3

17.47   Bach, Motet, *Jesu meine Freude*

C minor: V⁷/iv

17.48 Allegro   Bach, *Brandenburg Concerto No. 4*

17.49 Allegro molto   Spain

Schubert, *Valse sentimentale,* D. 779, No. 11

17.50

17.51 Canon for 3 voices   Byrd

Hey   ho!   to   the   Green - wood now   let   us

go. Sing heave _ and ho. And there will we

find both buck and doe. Sing heave and ho. The hart and

hind and the lit-tle pret - ty roe. Sing heave and ho.

* Canon may end at this point.

Section 4. Meters of 5 and 7, and other meters.

Gently (3 + 2)   Germany

17.52   *p*

Allegro (2 + 3)   Czechoslovakia

17.53   *f*

Andantino   Spain

17.54   *mp*

   mf

17.58 Canon for 3 voices — Germany

17.59 Pas vite — Chausson, *Le Colibri*

17.60 Allegretto / *simply and gracefully* — Bernstein, "The Ballad of Eldorado"

324

17.65 Allegro non troppo — Mexico — *mf*

17.66 Molto moderato — Elgar, *Caractacus* — *p*

O my war-ri-ors tell ___ me tru - ly ___

___ o'er the red graves where ___ ye lie. ___ That your

mon-arch led you du-ly, ___ first to charge ___ and last to fly. ___

___ O my war - - - ri - ors!

17.67 Molto moderato e pesante — Borodin, *Song of the Dark Forest* — *p*

17.68 Andante — Nova Scotia — *mf*

17.72 Andantino (♩ = 84) Moussorgsky, *Boris Godunov*

17.73 Adagio Spain

Section 5. Structured improvisation.

➤➤ Continue this melody using mostly stepwise motion and the leap of a third between the last two notes of every measure. Try to sustain the rhythm of constant eighth notes throughout. (You may prefer to deviate from established patterns in the last measure, however.)

17.74

➤➤ Elaborate the harmony indicated below each bracket using passing tones and chordal skips similar to the first measure. Although you should incorporate similar features in order to create the sense of a unified phrase, you do not have to adhere to a single repeating contour or rhythm. Notice that the meter consistently alternates between $\frac{3}{4}$ and $\frac{2}{4}$.

17.75

➤➤ Improvise a consequent phrase to answer the antecedent phrase provided below. Try to begin the second phrase with contrasting material, but be careful to maintain the established hemiola pattern throughout. End with a very strong cadential gesture so that the final cadence sounds more conclusive than the cadence in measure 4.

17.76

18

RHYTHM AND MELODY

further subdivision of the beat;
notation in slow tempi

The use of note values smaller than the divisions presented in previous chapters is relatively uncommon. Divisions smaller than those shown below are possible, but they are rarely used.

1. The beat note is divided into eight parts in simple meters and into twelve parts in compound meters. In signatures with other denominators, the beat note may be similarly divided.

For these divisions to be performed using the usual note value for one beat (as indicated by the meter signature), the tempo must be moderate to slow, but not as slow as described in 2.

2. The division of the beat (as indicated by the meter signature) is used as the beat-note value. When the tempo of a composition is very slow, the meter signature often does not actually express the number of beats in the measure. In a very slow $\frac{2}{4}$ measure, for example, there may actually be four beats, the eighth note receiving one beat. Similarly, in a very slow tempo, the numerator of the meter signature for a compound meter may actually indicate the number of

beats in the measure. Consequently, in a slow $\frac{6}{8}$, instead of two $\downarrow$. beats in one measure, there might be six $\downarrow$ beats in one measure.

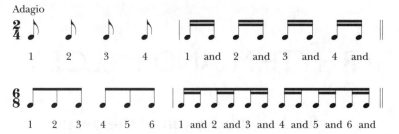

When to use the beat division as the actual beat note is sometimes difficult to ascertain. Beginning with Beethoven, who first made use of the metronome, composers at times include a metronome marking for the beat division, as in melody 18.22, where the eighth note receives the beat in $\frac{3}{4}$ time, and in melody 18.23, where the subdivision, a sixteenth note, is designated as the beat in $\frac{2}{4}$ time.

When no marking is supplied by the composer, an editorial marking in parentheses is sometimes included in the score, as in melody 18.26. Such a marking is based on the composer's tempo indication or determined through knowledge of the composer's style and of historical performance precedents. When not indicated, the beat-note value must be similarly determined by the performer. But there will always be borderline cases where a slight difference in opinion can result in a different choice of beat-note value.

Section I. Rhythmic reading.

Read each example, using these metronome markings:

18.1–18.6: M.M. $\downarrow$ = 50
18.7–18.8: M.M. $\downarrow$ = 50
18.9–18.11: M.M. $\downarrow$ = 44

Read each example again, using these metronome markings:

18.1–18.6: M.M. $\downarrow$ = 76
18.7–18.8: M.M. $\downarrow$ = 76
18.9–18.11: M.M. $\downarrow$ = 86

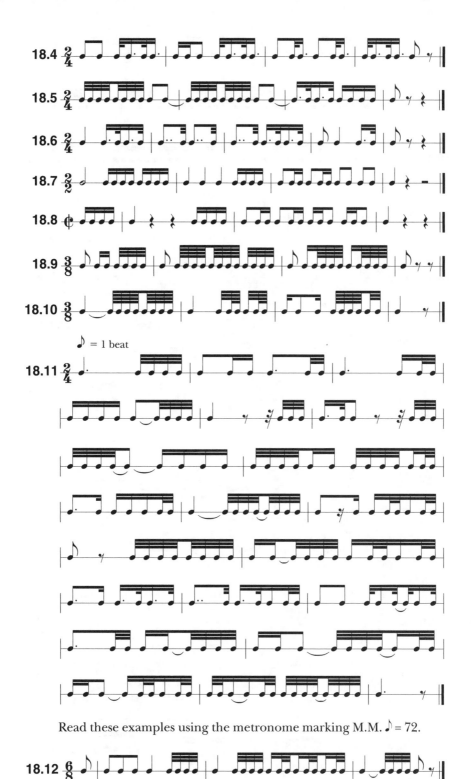

Read these examples using the metronome marking M.M. ♪ = 72.

Section 2. Sight singing.

18.19 Adagio — Haydn, Symphony No. 57

18.20 Moderato — Haydn, String Quartet, Op. 17, No. 5

18.21 Adagio — Haydn, Symphony No. 60

Andante cantabile (♪ = 80)

Donizetti, *Don Pasquale*

18.26

18.27 Handel, *Athalia*

Largo ($\quarternote$ = 72)

Section 3. Structured improvisation.

➤➤ Maintaining a very slow tempo, construct a modulating phrase that follows the harmonic profile below. In general, elaboration such as passing tones and neighboring tones should fall on weak beats, while strong beats should emphasize chord tones. Try to cadence on the new tonic.

18.35

G: I   vi   ii   V⁷   I   vi
                                   D: ii   V⁷   I

➤➤ Two common cadential bass formulas appear below. Elaborate each basic framework with neighboring tones, passing tones to other chord members, and occasional chordal skips. Some chords are open to interpretation (for instance, the B♭ in the first bass line might suggest iv or ii°⁶). Maintain a very slow tempo, and try to include some short note values such as ♪ and ♪.

18.36

18.37

19

MELODY

Chromaticism (III)

additional uses of chromatic tones; remote modulation

Section 1. Chromatic tones in less common intervals.

The chromaticism in these melodies produces intervals not frequently used. A few examples are the diminished third (19.1), the augmented fifth (19.3), the diminished fourth (19.5), and the minor ninth (19.6).

Rossini, *La donna del lago*

19.1

Moderato

Leo Wood, "Somebody Stole My Gal"

19.2

Allegro moderato

Haydn, String Quartet, Op. 77, No. 2

19.3

sotto voce

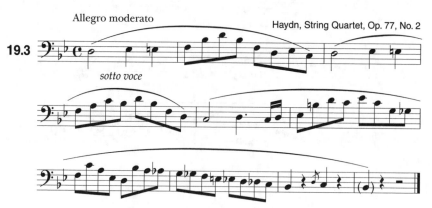

Canon for 3 voices

19.7   Couperin

Andante   Handel, *Imineo*

19.8

Schumann, String Quartet, Op. 40, No. 1

19.9

Wolf, *Nimmersatte Liebe*

19.10

Canon for 3 voices

19.11

Haydn

Section 2. The Neapolitan sixth.

The distinctive chromatic melody tone $\flat\hat{2}$ usually implies the use of a major triad whose root lies a minor second above the tonic (in C major or C minor, D♭–F–A♭). In harmonic study, this chord is commonly known as the Neapolitan triad (the origin of the name is unknown) and may be represented by the symbol "♭II" or "N." The chord is typically found in first inversion (♭II⁶ or N⁶) and leads to the dominant, either directly, through a cadential $\frac{6}{4}$ chord, or through vii°⁷/V.

In melodic writing, examples of the Neapolitan triad as three successive tones are not common. Nevertheless, example 19.12 shows the complete triad in both ascending and descending form; see also example 19.18.

It is more common in melodic writing to use only the most characteristic tone, $\flat\hat{2}$, or to use two tones, one of which is $\flat\hat{2}$. In such cases, it is usually the harmonic context that identifies the triad's presence. In the second phrase of example 19.13, the downward movement of $\flat\hat{2}$ to $\sharp\hat{7}$ (A♭–F♯, a diminished third) indicates the probable harmony as $\flat$II^6 resolving to V. Similarly, in example 19.17, measure 7, the interval E♭–C♯ suggests a progression from the Neapolitan to the dominant in D major. The preceding F♯ indicates a secondary dominant tonicizing the Neapolitan triad (B♭ D F→E♭ G B♭→ A C♯ E).

19.14 Grazioso   Rimsky-Korsakov, *The Snow Maiden*

pp

19.15 Allegro ben moderato   Meyerbeer, *L'Africaine*

f

19.16 Moderato   Sicily

mf

348

Ziemlich lebhaft

Schumann, *Des Sängers Fluchs,* Op. 139

19.20

Bach, Mass in B Minor, *Agnus Dei,* BWV 232

19.21

Tempo risoluto

Schumann, String Quartet, Op. 41, No. 3

19.22

sempre *f*

Section 3. Remote modulation.

A modulation to any key other than a closely related key is known as a *remote* (or *foreign*, or *distant*) modulation.

19.24

Langsam

Schubert, *Wehmut,* Op. 22, No. 2

19.25

Mässig

Schubert, *Jüngling am Bache,* Op. 87, No. 3

Moderato poco animato

Saint-Saëns, *Les Barbares*

19.29

Moderato poco allegretto

Mussorgsky, *Khovanschchina*

19.30

f

p

f

Andante poco mosso

Offenbach, *Tales of Hoffman*

19.31

p

poco animato

f   *allarg.*   **ff**   *Lento*

a tempo   **pp**

rall.

355

dim.

cresc.   *f*   *p*

p

cresc.   *f*   sempre *f*

p

dolce

Andantino maestoso   Rossini, *Le Chant des Titons*

19.34

19.35 Schubert, Waltz, Op. 9, No. 14
Waltz tempo

19.36 Schumann, *Dein Angesicht*, Op. 127, No. 2
Langsam

Borodin, *Song of the Dark Forest*

19.37

Schubert, Mass in A♭ Major

19.38

Section 4. Structured improvisation.

➤➤ Improvise a consequent phrase to answer the antecedent phrase provided below. Maintain a similar rhythmic profile, and try to incorporate several chromatic notes—particularly those borrowed from the parallel minor key.

19.39

➤➤ Elaborating the harmonic framework indicated below, improvise two four-measure phrases with an antecedent-consequent relationship.

19.40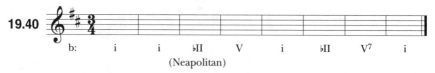

b: i   i   ♭II   V   i   ♭II   V⁷   i
              (Neapolitan)

➤➤ Improvise a modulating melody following the harmonic outline provided below. At first, you may want to restrict yourself to simple arpeggiations around the key change. Once the progression becomes more familiar, you will be able to elaborate all of the chords more consistently.

19.41

C: I   V⁷   I   ♭II
               A♭: IV   V⁷   I   IV V⁷   I

20

MELODY

the diatonic modes

The term *mode* refers to the arrangement of whole steps and half steps (or sometimes other intervals) to form a scale. In contrast to the present common use of major and minor modes, pre-seventeenth-century music was largely based on a system of six modes. These modes are also very common in folk music of the Western world. They were virtually neglected by composers of the seventeenth, eighteenth, and nineteenth centuries, but have again found favor in the twentieth and twenty-first centuries with composers of both serious and popular music.

The modes used in this chapter are those known variously as the *diatonic modes*, the *church modes*, the *ecclesiastical modes*, or the *medieval modes*.

Mode	White-note scale on keyboard[1]	Characteristic
Aeolian	A	Same as natural (pure) minor
Ionian	C	Same as major
Dorian	D	Similar to natural minor but with a raised sixth scale step
Phrygian	E	Similar to natural minor with a lowered second scale step
Lydian	F	Similar to major with a raised fourth scale step
Mixolydian	G	Similar to major with a lowered seventh scale step

[1] The mode on B, sometimes called *Locrian*, was not useful because of the interval of a tritone between tonic and dominant.

As an example, the Dorian mode can be realized by playing on the piano an ascending scale consisting of white keys only, starting on D. This results in a scale whose pattern of whole steps and half steps differs from the patterns of the well-known major and minor scales. This Dorian scale sounds somewhat like a minor scale but differs from D minor in that the sixth scale step is B♮ rather than B♭. The Dorian mode on D, therefore, has a signature of no sharps and no flats, although it is often found with a signature of one flat (D minor), with B♮ indicated throughout the composition.

Modes can be transposed to begin on any pitch or letter name. To transpose the Dorian mode to G, as in melody 20.6, note that the minor mode on G has two flats; raising the sixth scale step cancels the E♭, leaving one flat (B♭) in the scale. Usually the key signature uses those sharps or flats needed for its scale. In melody 20.20, the mode is Dorian on E; the key signature is two sharps, accommodating the C♯ found in this scale—E F♯ G A B C♯ D E. The signature of the parallel major or minor key may also be used. In melody 20.21, the mode is Mixolydian on A♭. The key signature is four flats, that of a major key on A♭. In the melody, a flat is added before each G($\hat{7}$)—A♭ B♭ C D♭ E♭ F G♭ A♭.

A modal melody can be found with one or more scale steps not used, making positive identification of the mode impossible. A melody with the tonic note D, using the pitches D E F G A–C D, could be Dorian with B missing or transposed Aeolian with B♭ missing (see melody 20.7).

Section 1. Folk music.

Aeolian mode: A B C D E F G A

Dorian mode: D E F G A B C D

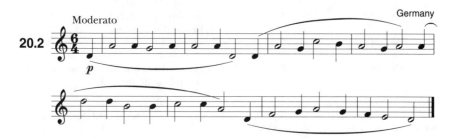

Phrygian mode: E F G A B C D E

20.3 Allegretto — Anon. (13th century)

Lydian: F G A B C D E F

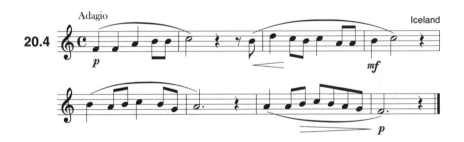

20.4 Adagio — Iceland

Mixolydian: G A B C D E F G

20.5 Allegro — England

Dorian, transposed: G A B♭ C D E F G

20.6   Allegro   England

Scale without 6̂: D E F G A–C D

20.7   Slow   Newfoundland

20.8   Con moto   Massachusetts

In number 20.15, $\hat{7}$ is raised when progressing directly or indirectly to the tonic tone.

20.19 Allegro ... Spain

20.20 Alla marcia ... France

20.21 Adagio   Scotland

Fine

D. C. al Fine

20.22 Moderato   Spain

20.23 Con moto   Newfoundland

20.24 Allegro moderato   England

Section 2. Composed music.

In pre-seventeenth-century composed music, notes were sometimes altered by means of a device known as *musica ficta* ("feigned music"). Although the accidentals were not actually written, performers recognized that certain chromatic inflections were implied by the composer (either for aesthetic or practical reasons, such as avoiding augmented or diminished intervals). One particularly common example occurs at cadences: if $\hat{7}$ falls a whole step below $\hat{1}$, it is frequently raised a half step (comparable to the later practice of raising $\hat{7}$ in minor keys). In modern editions, an accidental is written *above* the note that was probably intended to be altered. Applying *musica ficta* affects the music's performance, but the mode is considered unchanged, as shown below.

Jacobus Vaet, *Ave Maris Stella*

20.27

Willaert, *Allons, allons gay*

20.28

Music by Alec Rowley. Words by Guida Crowley.
Copyright © 1954 (Renewed) by Novello & Company, Ltd.
International Copyright Secured. All Rights Reserved. Used by permission.

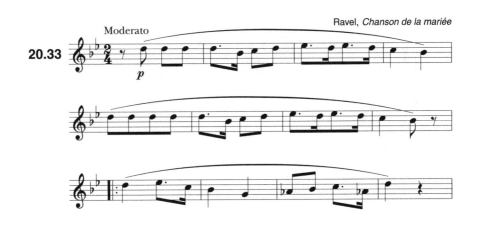

20.34 Vincenzo Galilei, *Contrapuncti*

20.35 Lassus, *Crucifixus*

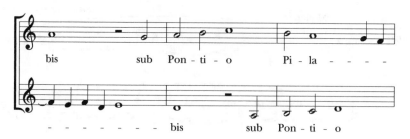

Cru – ci – fi – xus e – ti – am pro – no –

Cru – ci – fi – xus e – ti – am pro – no –

bis sub Pon – ti – o Pi – la – – –

– – – – – – bis sub Pon – ti – o

- - - - - to pas - sus et se - pul - tus est.

Pi - la - to pas - sus et - - - - se - pul - tus est.

Josquin, *Missa ad Fugam*

20.36

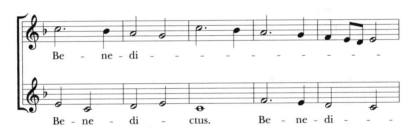

Be - ne - di - ctus, be - ne - di - ctus.

Be - ne - di - ctus.

Be - ne - di - - - - - - - - - - - -

Be - ne - di - ctus. Be - ne - di - - -

ctus, be - ne - di - - - - ctus.

- - - - - - - - - ctus.

di Lasso, *Bicinien*, No. 18

20.37

Victoria, Magnificat Septimi Toni

20.38

et ex - al - ta - vit hu - - - mi -

et ex - al - ta - vit hu - mi - -

et ex - al - ta - vit hu - mi -

Palestrina, *Missa de Beata Virgine*

20.39

20.40

Largo *p*

Tallis (1567), *Why Fumeth in Sight?*

(Melody in Tenor)*

Why fumeth in sight the Gen - tiles spite: in fu - ry rag - ing stout. Why tak'th in hand the peo - ple fond, vain things to bring a - bout. The kings a - rise, the lords de - vise in coun - cils

*This melody is used by Ralph Vaughan Williams in his *Fantasia on a Theme of Thomas Tallis.*

met there - to.   A - gainst   the   Lord   with

false   ac - cord   a - gainst his   Christ they   go.

Section 3. Structured improvisation.

▶▶ Using entirely stepwise motion, follow the suggested rhythm to create a G Dorian melody. Plan ahead so that you will end on G. (Note: You may wish to repeat this exercise in different modes.)

20.41

▶▶ Complete the partial melody below, including a balanced mixture of stepwise motion and leaps. A rhythm has been suggested. Be careful not to stray from the Mixolydian mode.

20.42

▶▶ Improvise a consequent phrase to answer the antecedent phrase provided below. Be careful to maintain the Aeolian mode, and focus on approaching the final D in a properly cadential manner.

20.43

21

RHYTHM AND MELODY

the twentieth century

Presented in this chapter is a short introductory study of rhythmic and melodic writing in the twentieth century. During that time and into the twenty-first century, most composers of "serious music" have turned away from the precepts and methods of the preceding 300 years (Bach through Wagner), and instead have explored many new ways of expressing themselves in melody, harmony, and rhythm. The result has been a large catalogue of varying compositional styles, in contrast to the single "common practice" style featured in earlier chapters. The music examples that follow illustrate some of the new concepts that many such composers have developed in order to achieve basic characteristics differing from those of earlier periods.

Section 1. Meter and rhythm. Rhythmic reading.

Meter in music is no longer bound to a system of regular recurring accents and an equal number of beats in each measure. As an example, changing meters and less common meter signatures, similar to those seen in Chapter 17, are widely used. In any meter, bar lines no longer necessarily imply regularly recurring strong and weak beats, nor do meter signatures necessarily indicate the location of primary accents. Rhythmic patterns can be indicated by beaming of note values, phrase marks, and other notational devices. Bar lines, then, often function simply as a guide to the eye.

The rhythmic reading examples in this chapter illustrate some of the rhythmic and metrical practices that arose in the twentieth century and are not typical of common-practice music.

* No meter signature

383

Carter

21.10

Schoenberg

21.11

Section 2. Extensions of the traditional tonal system.

Tonality did not by any means disappear at the end of the nineteenth century. However, many composers began to use traditional tonal features more flexibly. For instance, some music employs familiar diatonic collections without projecting a functional harmonic progression in the background (21.13), while other music provides fleeting glimpses of conventional harmony in the context of a rapidly shifting tonal center (21.29). Sometimes the melody seems to obscure the underlying harmony (21.21), suggesting a kind of hazy tonality where we can only barely recognize customary elements through the blurred sonic image.

To sight sing these melodies, first scan them for passages where the diatonic collection and/or the underlying harmony is clear. During these sections, it is appropriate to apply the solmization system you prefer for more traditional tonal music. When the collection or tonal center changes suddenly, focus on rapidly shifting the syllables. (This procedure will be familiar from navigating modulations in previous chapters.) When you encounter more ambiguous segments, employ a tonally neutral strategy such as intervals or letter names.

Canon for 4 voices
Con slancio

Benjamin Britten, *Peter Grimes*

21.12

Old Joe has gone fish-ing and young Joe has gone fish-ing, and

you know has gone fish-ing and found them a shoal.___

Pull them in in hand-fuls and in can-fuls and in

pan-fulls, Bring them in sweet-ly. Gut them com-

plete-ly, Pack them up neat-ly, Sell them dis-

creet-ly, O haul ___ a-way! ___

___ O haul ___ a-way!

Aaron Copland, *Twelve Poems of Emily Dickinson,*
"The Chariot"

With quiet grace

21.13

mp   mf

mp

more slowly mf

21.14

Assez vif et triste

Ned Rorem, *Poemès pour la paix*, "Sonnet"

21.15 Samuel Barber, *Monks and Raisins*

Allegro

mp

p

Composed by Samuel Barber, Words by Jose Garcia Villa and Robert Horan. Copyright © 1944
(Renewed) by G. Schirmer, Inc. (ASCAP). International Copyright Secured. All Rights Reserved.
Reprinted by permission

21.16 Kern, "Till the Clouds Roll By"

Allegretto

21.17 Seymour Barab, *A Child's Garden of Verses*

Vivace

mf

p

cresc.

f

21.18

Maurice Ravel, *Schéhérazade*

Allegro

rall.

Trés lent

Modéré

© 1909 Durand S.A. Used by permission. Sole Representative U.S.A. Thodore Presser Company.

21.19

Béla Bartók, String Quartet No. 3

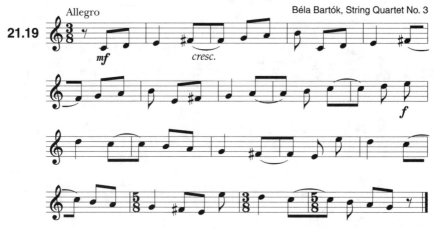

Allegro

© Copyright 1929 by Boosey & Hawkes, Inc., for the USA only. Copyright Renewed. Reprinted by permission.

Claude Debussy, *Fêtes Galantés,* "Fantoches"
(Orig.: Perfect 4th higher)

Allegretto scherzando

21.20

Rêveusement lent

Debussy, *En Sourdine*

21.21

poco cresc.

Lent

21.22

Fast

Samuel Adler, *Nothing Is Enough!*

Dominick Argento, *Postcard from Morocco*

Meno mosso ♩ = 76

21.23

♩ = 80

Molto tranquillo (♩ = 66)

Weill, "Liebeslied"

21.24

Lively and rhythmic

Benjamin Britten, *Midsummer Night's Dream*

21.25

You spot-ted snakes with dou-ble tongue.

Thorn-y hedge - hogs be not seen, Newts and blind worms

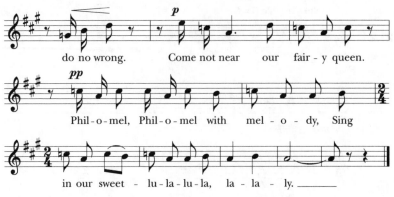

do no wrong.　Come not near　our　fair - y queen.

Phil - o - mel, Phil - o - mel with　mel - o - dy, Sing

in our sweet - lu - la - lu - la,　la - la - ly.

Flowing　　　　　　　　　　　　Paul Hindemith, *Das Marienleben*, Op. 27

21.26

Martin Mailman, *Geometrics No. 4,*
Op. 43 (for band)
(Orig.: 1 or 2 octaves higher)

Allegro moderato

21.30

Agitato ($\quad$ = 126)

William Walton, *Troilus and Cressida*

21.31

*May sing an octave lower from this point.

Allegro gioviale

William Walton, *Partita for Orchestra*

21.32

21.33

© *Copyright 1908, 1909 by Adolph Furstner. Copyright Renewed. Copyright assigned 1943 to Hawkes & Son (London) Ltd. (a Boosey & Hawkes company) for the world excluding Germany, Italy, Portugal and the former territories of the U.S.S.R (excluding Estonia, Latvia, and Lithuania). Reprinted by permission of Boosey & Hawkes, Inc.*

21.34

Paul Hindemith, *Mathis der Maler*

21.35

Dmitri Shostakovitch, Symphony No. 10

21.36

21.37 Béla Bartók, String Quartet No. 6

Molto vivace

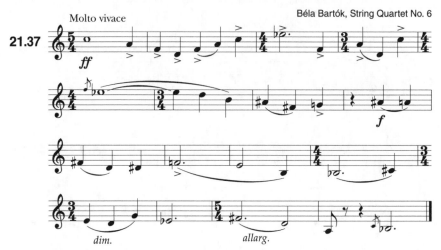

21.38 Arthur Honegger, *Pacific 231*

Rhythmique $\quad \downarrow = 80$

marcato

21.39 Bartók, "My Love," Op. 15

Parlando ($\downarrow$ = 69–63)

Section 3. Symmetrical collections; the whole-tone and octatonic scales.

A substantial number of post-tonal compositions use special collections that are often described as *modes of limited transposition* or *transpositionally symmetrical scales*. These scales are constructed using a repeating interval pattern (such as M2–M2–M2–M2–M2 or M2–m2–M2–m2–M2–m2–M2–m2, as seen below); consequently, they produce an equivalent collection when transposed by some intervals (unlike the diatonic scale, which has twelve distinct transpositions). Two of the most important examples are shown here.

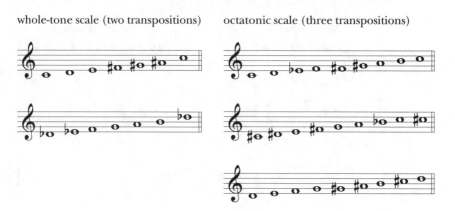

whole-tone scale (two transpositions)   octatonic scale (three transpositions)

Just as identifying diatonic segments facilitates rapid and accurate sight singing of tonal and quasi-tonal literature, recognizing whole-tone and octatonic passages can lead to superior sight singing of certain post-tonal literature. To take advantage of this knowledge, however, a musician must first be able to sing the scales fluently.

The melodies in this section include at least one passage based on a mode of limited transposition. Before you begin sight singing, scan the melodies for passages involving a familiar collection (whole tone, octatonic, or diatonic). Actively concentrating on the distinctive sound and characteristic intervals of each scale will help to keep you oriented during these portions of the melody.

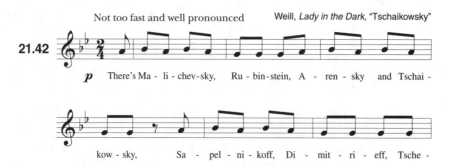

Not too fast and well pronounced   Weill, *Lady in the Dark*, "Tschaikowsky"

21.42

p There's Ma - li - chev-sky, Ru - bin-stein, A - ren - sky and Tschai -

kow - sky, Sa - pel - ni - koff, Di - mit - ri - eff, Tsche -

rep-nin, Kry-ja - now-sky,   Go - dow-sky, Ar - tei - bou-cheff, Mo - ni -

usz-ko, A - ki - men-ko,   So - lo - vi - eff, Pro - ko - fi - eff, Ti -

om-kin, Ko - rest - chen - ko.   There's   Glin - ka,   Win - kler,

mp

Bort - ni - an-sky,   Re - bi-koff, Il - yin - sky,   There's   Medt-ner,   Ba - la -

kir - eff,   Zo - lo - tar - eff   and   Kvo - schin - sky.

Debussy, *Fêtes Gallantes II*, "Colloque Sentimentale"

Triste et lent

21.43

p   *p*   *p*   molto dim - - - - -

pp

Plus lent (60 = ♩)   Nadia Boulanger, "Elégie"

21.44

rit.

21.45 Modéré (mais sourdement agité)   Claude Debussy, *Fêtes Galantes II*, "De Grève"

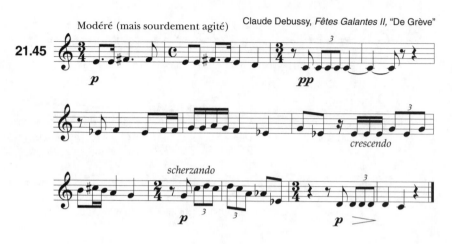

crescendo

scherzando

21.46 Modéré   Debussy, *Fêtes Galantes II*, "Les Ingénus"

21.47 Très lent   Ravel, "Si Morne"

21.48

Modéré   Messiaen, *Poémes pour mi*, "Épouvante"

21.49

Allegro molto ♩. = 104   Lutoslawski, "Bukoliki"

Presque lent ($\flat$ = 66)

Messiaen, *Poémes pour mi,* "Ta voix"

21.50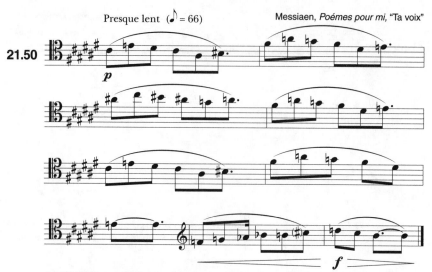

Bien modéré

Messiaen, *Poémes pour mi,* "Prière exaucée"

21.51

Section 4. Freely post-tonal melodies; twelve-tone melodies.

The melodies in this section are freely chromatic, not oriented around conventional harmonic progressions or widely recognized scales (other than the chromatic scale). Sight singing them requires a flexible strategy: scan a melody for short segments that form a subset of a familiar collection, repeat a prominent motive, emphasize a specific interval, and so on. In order to take full advantage of your many skills, you may need to change your focus judiciously from moment to moment in response to the changing context.

21.52   Andante amoroso   Alban Berg, *Lyrische Suite*

21.53   Allegro giusto   Elliott Carter, Piano Sonata

21.54   ♩ = 100   Thomas Clark, *Isostrata*

Luigi Dallapiccola, *Cinque Frammenti de Saffo*
(Orig.: Major 3rd higher)

21.55 Largo

Arnold Schoenberg, *Schenk mir deinen goldenen Kamm,* Op. 2, No. 2 (1900)

21.56 Sehr langsam

Anton Webern, *Gesang einer gefangenen Amsel,* Op. 14, No. 6

21.57 Sehr fliessende Achtel

21.58

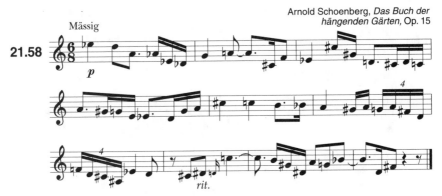

21.59

Twelve-tone (or *dodecaphonic*) music derives its material from a twelve-tone *row* (or *series*), which is an ordering of all twelve distinct pitch classes.[1] Composers typically transform the original row using a variety of operations, including transposition, inversion, and retrograde.[2] If you examine the next

---

[1] The designation *serial music* is more general, referring to compositions based on an ordered series of any length. Although the ordering usually affects pitch, it could also involve durations, dynamics, orchestration, or any other musical parameter.

[2] Inversion and retrograde may be informally described as "upside down" and "backwards," respectively.

several melodies, you will find that each one begins with a presentation of the complete chromatic collection. Melody 21.60 contains only one statement of the row, but in melodies 21.61 and 21.62 you should be able to determine a specific relationship between the different row forms.

Notice that composers sometimes repeat notes within a row, and appearances of the row do not necessarily correspond with musical phrases. Can you guess the next few notes that follow the excerpt in melody 21.62?

Jel - ly - beans___ glowed___ in the

sem-i___ gloom___ of that Sep-tem-ber___ af - ter - noon.___

Section 5. Duets.

Jack Beeson, *Lizzie Borden*

21.64

Tranquillo (♩ = 56)

Strings

Harp

Ralph Vaughan Williams, Symphony in E Minor
(1948)*

*In the composer's score, the part for harp is a series of block chords. Given here is the lowest note of each chord transposed up one octave, with added figured bass symbols to indicate chord spellings. Play the complete harmony on the piano while singing the melody.

21.65

♩. = 132

Stravinsky, *The Rake's Progress*

Glenn Caluda, *Four Introspections for Solo Guitar*

Expressive

21.66

Sostenuto ♩ = ca. 100

Witold Lutoslawski, "The Lime Tree in the Field"

21.67

21.68

Vif et joyeux

Naji Hakim, *Le Tombeau d'Olivier Messiaen*

mf legato

mf legato

Courtesy of Carl Fisher, LLC on behalf of United Music Publishers, Ltd. (Theodore Presser Company). © Copyright 1994. Reprinted by permission.

21.69

Allegro

Merrill Ellis, Quintet for Oboe and Strings

Vln. I

mf

Oboe

Vln. II

Vln. I

mp

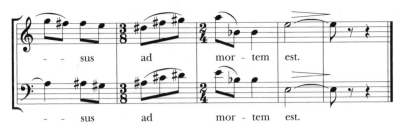

Dmitri Shostakovitch, Fugue No. 15, Op. 87

21.71

Section 6. Structured improvisation.

➤➤ The written portion of melody 21.73 revolves around one of the whole-tone collections. Complete it using only notes from the *other* whole-tone collection. Try to include at least one leap.

21.73

other whole-tone collection

▶▶ Continue the phrase, repeating the rhythmic pattern from measure 1 in measures 2 and 3. (You will probably want to change the rhythmic pattern in measure 4 to create a cadential effect.) In part *a*, restrict yourself to notes from the established whole-tone collection; in part *b*, maintain the octatonic collection.

21.74

(a) whole tone

(b) octatonic

▶▶ Improvise a phrase using only two intervals: the minor second and the major third. (Note: you may wish to repeat this exercise using other intervals.) An opening measure has been suggested.

21.75

APPENDIX:
MUSICAL TERMS

Most music commonly performed at the present time contains directions for performance, particularly in reference to tempo and dynamics. These markings were first added to music scores by a few Italian composers in the seventeenth century. As this procedure became more widespread, directions in Italian became standard in all languages. In the late nineteenth century, composers began using terms from their native languages, such as French, German, and English, though the older Italian terms continued to be commonly used.

This list presents a selection of terms frequently encountered in music, including all terms found in *Music for Sight Singing*. The language is Italian unless otherwise indicated: (F) = French, (G) = German, (L) = Latin.

a, à (F)   by
accelerando   getting faster
Achtel (G)   eighth note
adagietto   slightly faster than adagio
adagio   slow, leisurely
ad libitum (L)   at will (abbr. *ad lib*)
affetto   emotion, passion
affettuoso   very expressively
affretti   hurried
agitato   agitated
al   to
all', alla   to the, at the, in the, in the style of

allant (F)   stirring, bustling
allargando   growing broader, slowing down with fuller tone (abbr. *allarg.*)
allegretto   moderately fast; slower than allegro
allegro   lively, fast
all'ottava   perform an octave higher (when above the notes); perform an octave lower (when below the notes)
all'unisono   in unison
amoroso   amorous, loving
andante   moderately slow
andantino   slower than andante

animando   with growing animation
animato   animated
animé (F)   animated
a piacere   freely
appassionato   with passion
assai   very
assez (F)   enough, rather
a tempo   return to the original tempo
   after a change
attacca   begin next section at once
aussi (F)   as

belebter (G)   lively
ben   well
bewegt (G)   moved
bien (F)   well, very
brio   vivacity, spirit, fire
brioso   with fire, spiritedly

calando   decreasing
calme   calm
cantabile   in a singing style
coda   end of piece
col', coll', colla, colle   with
comodo, commodo   comfortable tempo
con   with
coulé (F)   smoothly
crescendo   increasing in volume
   (abbr. *cresc.*)

da capo   from the beginning
   (abbr. *D.C.*)
dal segno   from the sign (abbr. *D.S.*)
deciso   with decision
declamato   in declamatory style
decrescendo   decreasing in volume
   (abbr. *decresc.*)
di   of, from, to
diminuendo   decreasing in volume
   (abbr. *dim.*)
dolce   soft
dolcissimo   sweetly
dolendo   doleful, sad
dolore   pain, grief
doppio   double
douce, doux (F)   soft, sweet

e   and
einfach (G)   simple, plain
energico   energetic, vigorous
ernst (G)   earnest, serious
erregeter (G)   excited

espressivo   expressive (abbr. *espress.*)
et (F)   and
etwas (G)   somewhat

feierlich (G)   solemn
ferocé (F)   wild, fierce
fine   end
flebile   tearful, plaintive
fliessende (G)   flowing
forte   loud (abbr. *f*)
forte-piano   loud, then immediately
   soft (abbr. *fp*)
fortissimo   very loud (abbr. *ff*)
forzando   with force (abbr. *fz*)
frisch (G)   glad, joyous
frölich (G)   glad, joyous
fuoco   fire

gai (F)   gay, brisk
gaiment, gayment (F)   gaily, briskly
gavotte   French dance; moderate
   tempo, quadruple time
gesangvoll (G)   in a singing style
geschwind (G)   swift, rapid
giocoso   playful
giojoso   joyful, mirthful
gioviale   jovial, cheerful
giusto   correct
gracieusement (F)   graciously
gracieux (F)   gracious
grandioso   grand, pompous
grave   slow, ponderous
grazia   grace, elegance
grazioso   graceful
gut (G)   good, well
gut zu declamiren (G)   clearly declaimed

heimlich (G)   mysterious
herzlich (G)   heartily, affectionate

im (G)   in
immer (G)   always
innig (G)   heartfelt, fervent
Innigkeit (G)   deep emotion
istesso   same
istesso tempo   same tempo (after
   a change of time signature)

joyeux (F)   joyous

klagend (G)   mourning
kurz (G)   short, crisp

Ländler Austrian dance; slow, in triple time

langoureuse, langoureux (F) langourous

langsam (G) slow

langsamer (G) slower

languido languid

largamente broadly

larghetto not as slow as largo

larghissimo very slow

largo slow and broad, stately

lebhaft (G) lively, animated

legato smoothly connected

leger (F) light

leggiero light (abbr. *legg.*)

leicht (G) light

leise (G) soft

lent (F) slow

lentement (F) slowly

lenteur (F) slowness

lento slow

liberamente freely

lieblich (G) with charm

l'istesso tempo same as *istesso tempo*

lustig (G) merry, lusty

ma but

mächtig (G) powerful

mais sourdement agité (F) but secretly agitated

maestoso, with majesty or dignity

malinconico in a melancholy style

marcato marked, emphatic

marcia march

marziale martial

mässig (G) moderate

même (F) same

meno less

mesto sad

mezzo half (mezzo forte, *mf*; mezzo piano, *mp*)

misterioso mysteriously

mit (G) with

moderato moderately

modéré (F) moderate

modérément (F) moderately

molto much, very

morendo dying away

mosso "moved" (*meno mosso*, less rapid; *più mosso*, more rapid)

moto motion

munter (G) lively, animated

mutig (G) spirited, bold

nicht (G) not

niente nothing

non not

non tanto not so much

non troppo not too much

nobilimente with nobility

ossia or

ottava octave

parlando singing in a speaking style

pas (F) not

pastorale pastoral

pas trop lent (F) not too slow

pesante heavy

peu (F) little

peu à peu (F) little by little

pianissimo very soft (abbr. *pp*)

piano soft (abbr. *p*)

più more

plus (F) more

poco little

precipitando hasty, reckless

presque (F) almost

presto fast, rapid

prima, primo first

quasi as if, nearly (as in *andante quasi allegretto*)

rallentando slowing down (abbr. *rall.*)

rasch (G) quick

rêveusement lent pensively slow

rhythmique (F) rhythmic, strongly accented

rigaudon Provençal dance; moderate tempo, quadruple time

rinforzando reinforcing; sudden increase in loudness for a single tone, chord, or passage (abbr. *rfz.*)

risoluto strongly marked

ritardando slowing down (abbr. *rit.*)

rubato perform freely

ruhig (G) quiet

sanft (G) soft

sans (F) without

sarabande Spanish dance; slow tempo, triple time

scherzando playfully

schnell (G) fast

sec, secco dry

segue   follows; next section follows immediately; or, continue in a similar manner

sehr (G)   very

semplice   simple

semplicemente   simply

sempre   always

sentito   with feeling

senza   without

sforzando   forcing; perform a single note or chord with sudden emphasis (abbr. *sfz.*)

siciliano   Sicilian dance; moderate tempo, $\frac{6}{8}$ or $\frac{12}{8}$ meter

simile   similarly; continue in the same manner (abbr. *sim.*)

slancio   impetuousness

sostenuto   sustained

sotto   under

sotto voce   in an undertone; subdued volume

spirito, spiritoso   spirit

staccato   detached; with distinct breaks between tones

stark (G)   strong

stendendo   slowing down (abbr. *stent.*)

stringendo   pressing onward

subito   suddenly

tant (F)   as much

tanto   so much

tempo   time

tempo giusto   correct tempo

tendrement (F)   tenderly

teneramente   tenderly

tenuto   held

tranquillo   tranquil

traurig (G)   sad

très (F)   very

triste (F)   sad

tristezza   sadness, melancholy

trop (F)   too much

troppo   too much

un, uno   one, a, an

una corda   one string; on the piano: use soft pedal (abbr. *u.c.*)

und (G)   and

unisono   unison

vif (F)   lively

vite (F)   quick

vivace   very fast

vivamente   very fast

vivo   lively

volante (F)   flowing

zart (G)   tender, delicate

zartlich (G)   tenderly

ziemlich (G)   somewhat, rather

zierlich (G)   delicate, graceful

zögerend (G)   lingering